Utilize este código QR para se cadastrar de forma mais rápida:

Ou, se preferir, entre em:
www.richmond.com.br/ac/livroportal
e siga as instruções para ter acesso aos conteúdos exclusivos do
Portal e Livro Digital

CÓDIGO DE ACESSO:

A 00110 JBEANS 1 99622

Faça apenas um cadastro. Ele será válido para:

MODERNA Richmond SANTILLANA ESPAÑOL

24070731 JELLY BEANS 1

CB053073

Da semente ao livro,
sustentabilidade por todo o caminho

Plantar florestas
A madeira que serve de matéria-prima para nosso papel vem de plantio renovável, ou seja, não é fruto de desmatamento. Essa prática gera milhares de empregos para agricultores e ajuda a recuperar áreas ambientais degradadas.

Fabricar papel e imprimir livros
Toda a cadeia produtiva do papel, desde a produção de celulose até a encadernação do livro, é certificada, cumprindo padrões internacionais de processamento sustentável e boas práticas ambientais.

Criar conteúdos
Os profissionais envolvidos na elaboração de nossas soluções educacionais buscam uma educação para a vida pautada por curadoria editorial, diversidade de olhares e responsabilidade socioambiental.

Construir projetos de vida
Oferecer uma solução educacional Moderna é um ato de comprometimento com o futuro das novas gerações, possibilitando uma relação de parceria entre escolas e famílias na missão de educar!

MODERNA

Apoio: TWO SIDES
www.twosides.org.br

Fotografe o Código QR e conheça melhor esse caminho.
Saiba mais em *moderna.com.br/sustentavel*

Jelly beans

1

This is my book.

_____

Rebecca Williams & Adela Trabolsi

Student's Book

Richmond

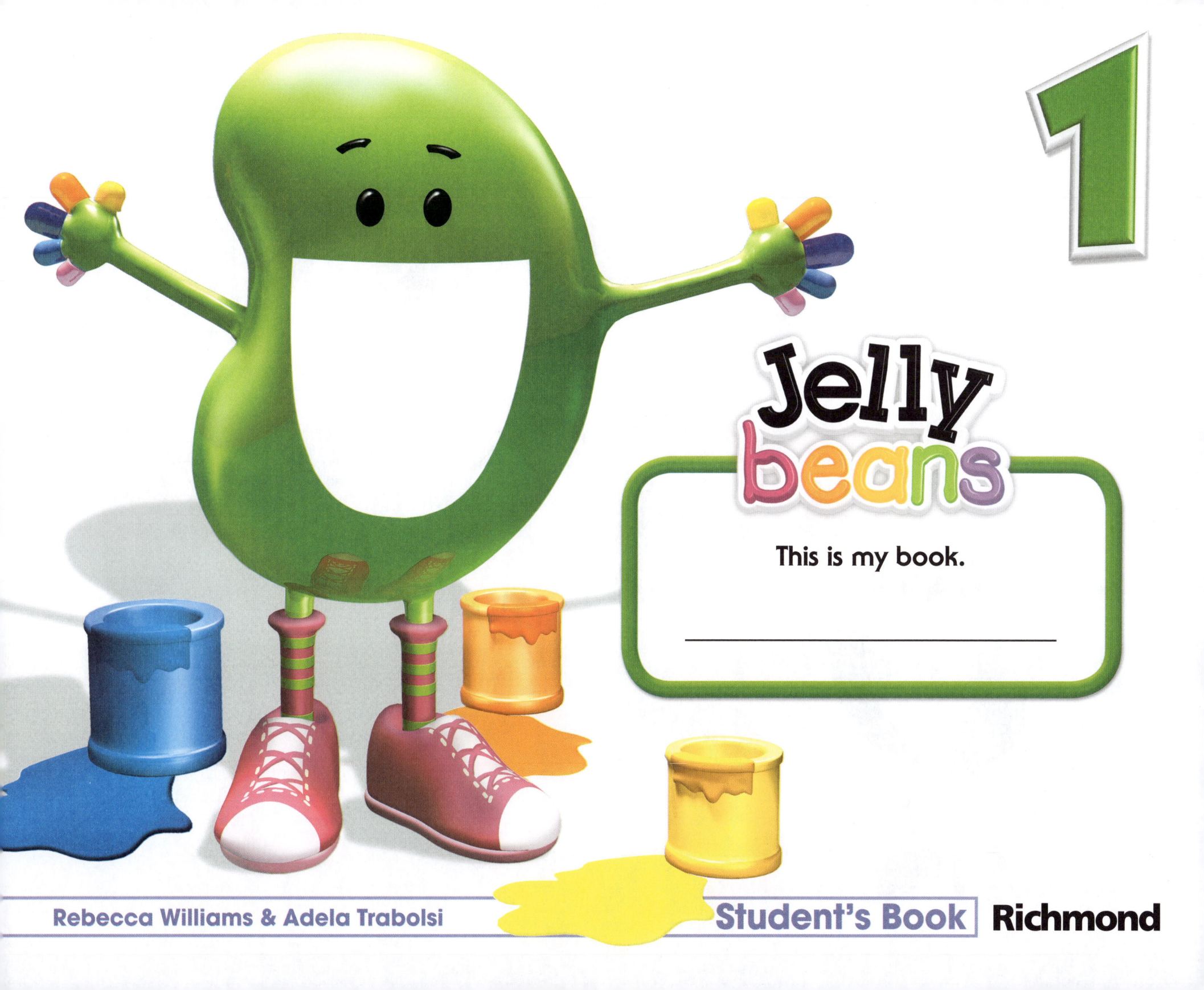

Anna

Ricky

Teacher

I go to school

Unit 1

Point and color.

Unit 1　**I go to school**　　Lesson 1

Look and stick.

Unit 1　**I go to school**　Lesson 1

Trace and color.

Unit 1 I go to school   Lesson 2

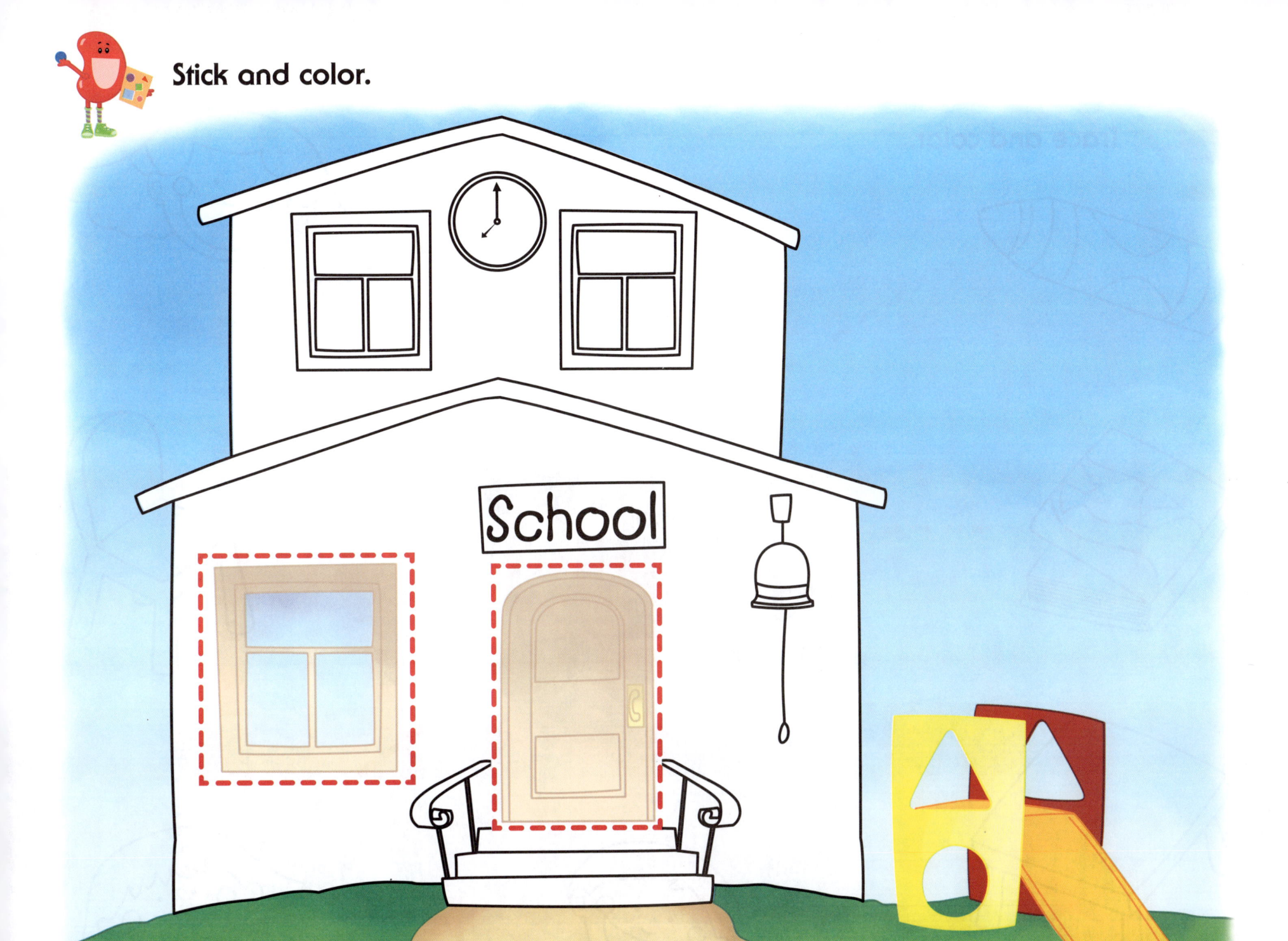

Stick and color.

Unit 1 **I go to school** Lesson 2

Trace and color.

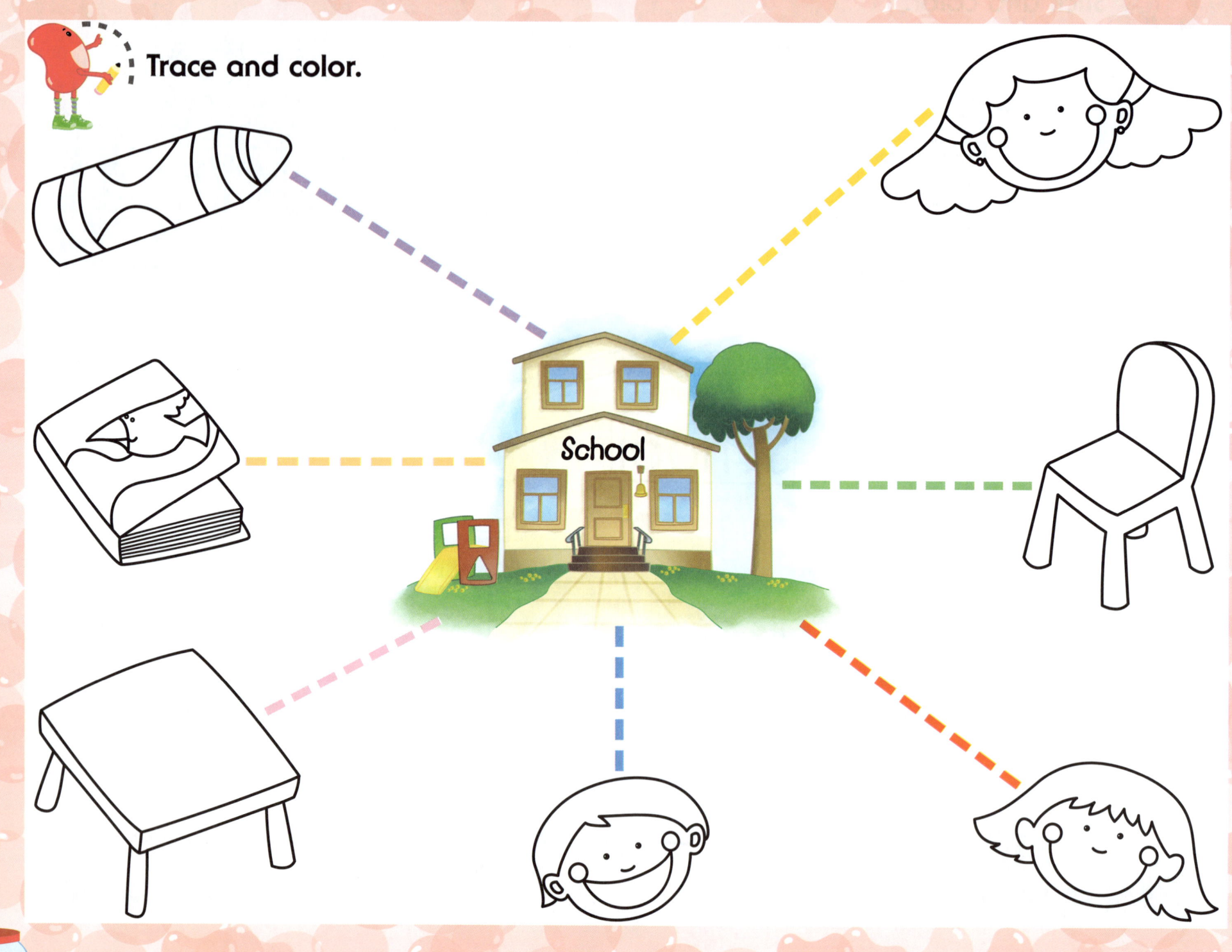

Unit 1 **I go to school** Review

Colors and numbers

Unit 2

Look and color.

Unit 2 Colors and numbers   Lesson 1

Trace and stick.

Unit 2 Colors and numbers Lesson 1

Look and color.

1

2

3

Unit 2 Colors and numbers   Lesson 2

Trace and stick.

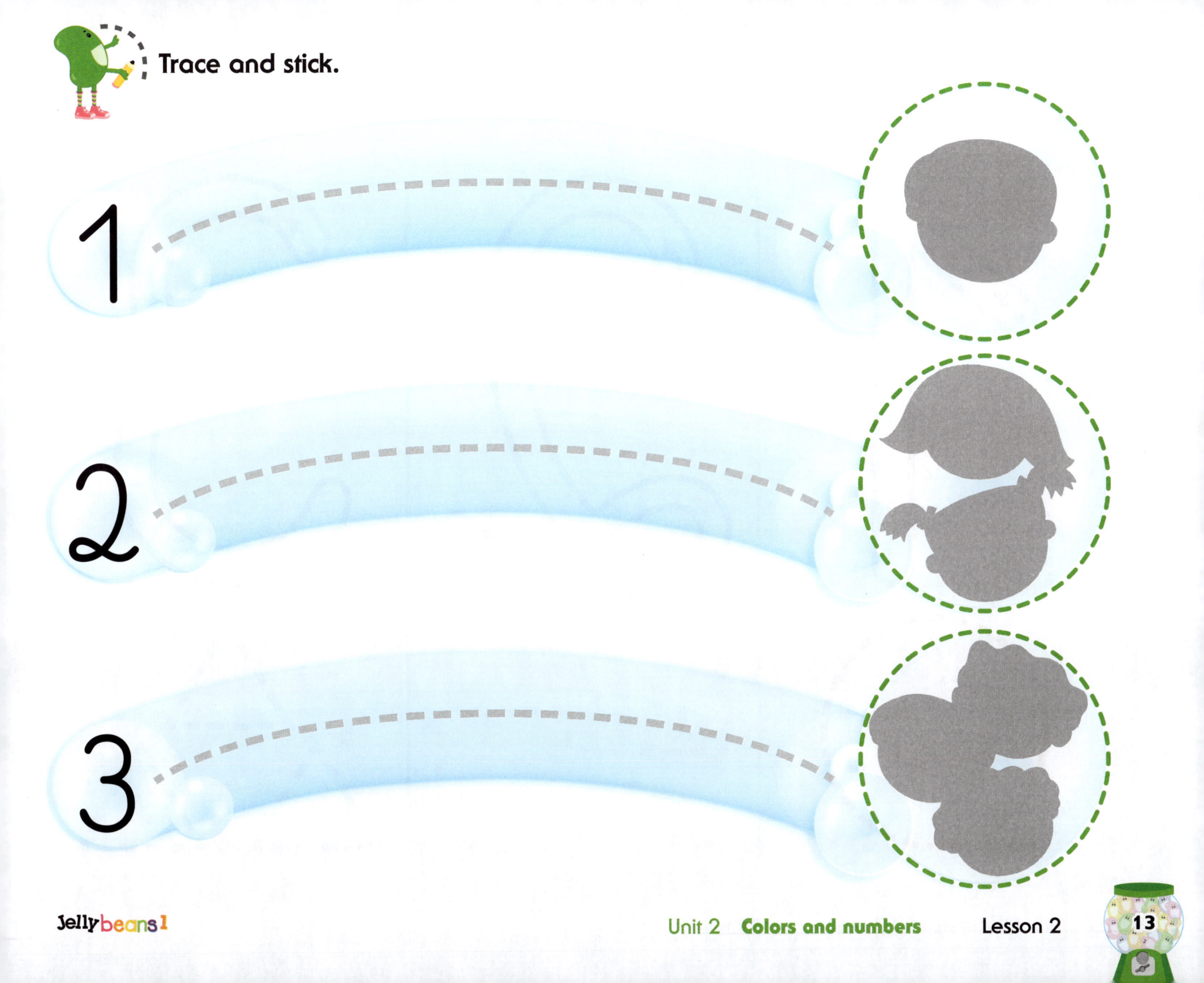

1

2

3

Unit 2 Colors and numbers   Lesson 2

Trace, count and color.

1 2 3

Unit 2 Colors and numbers Review

Unit 3

My face

Look and color.

16 Unit 3 **My face** Lesson 1

Look and stick.

Unit 3 My face   Lesson 1

Count and trace.

1

2

Unit 3 **My face**   Lesson 2

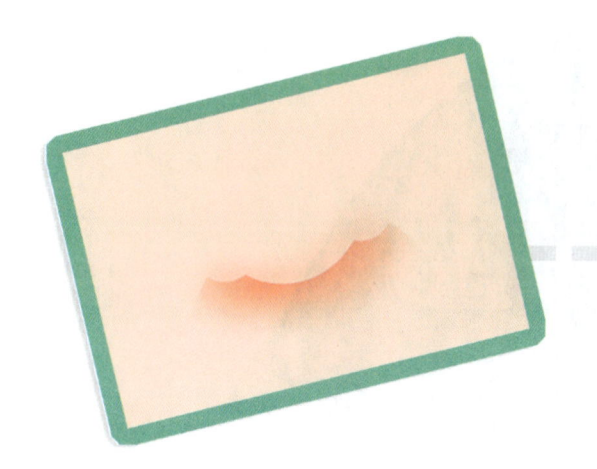

Look and stick.

Unit 3 My face Lesson 2

Look and color.

20 Unit 3 **My face** Review

My family

Unit 4

Point and color.

Unit 4 **My family**   Lesson 1

Stick and trace.

Unit 4 **My family** Lesson 1

Look, point and color.

Unit 4   **My family**   Lesson 2

Look, say and stick.

Unit 4   My family   Lesson 2

Point and circle.

26 Unit 4 **My family** Review

Unit 5

Nature

Trace and stick.

Unit 5 **Nature** Lesson 1

Look and color.

Trace and color.

Unit 5 **Nature** Lesson 2

Point, name and stick.

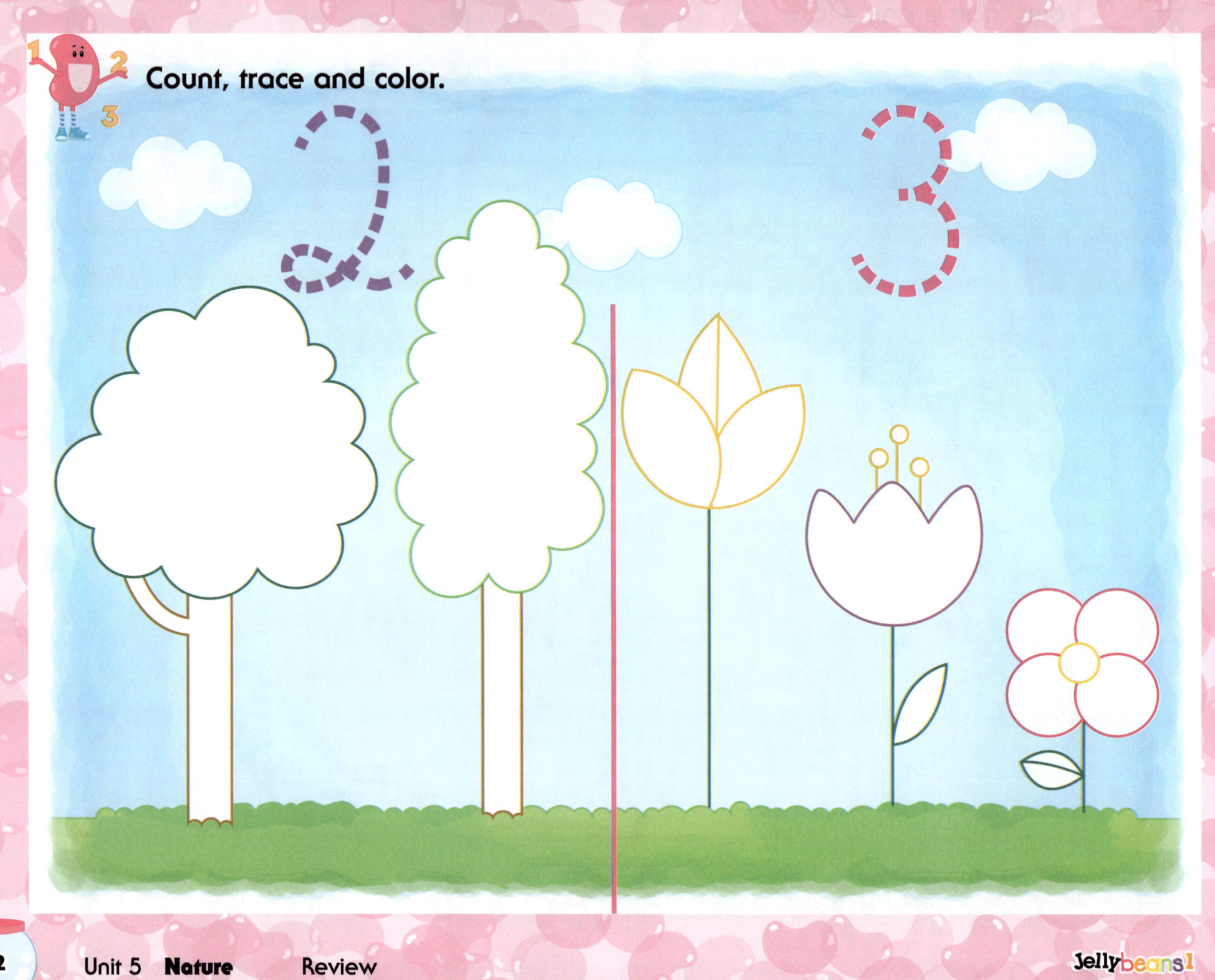

Count, trace and color.

Pets

Unit 6

Look and stick.

Unit 6 Pets   Lesson 1

Look and color.

1 = 🟤   2 = 🟢   3 = ⚫   4 = ⚪

Point, match and color.

Unit 6 Pets   Lesson 2

Count, stick and trace.

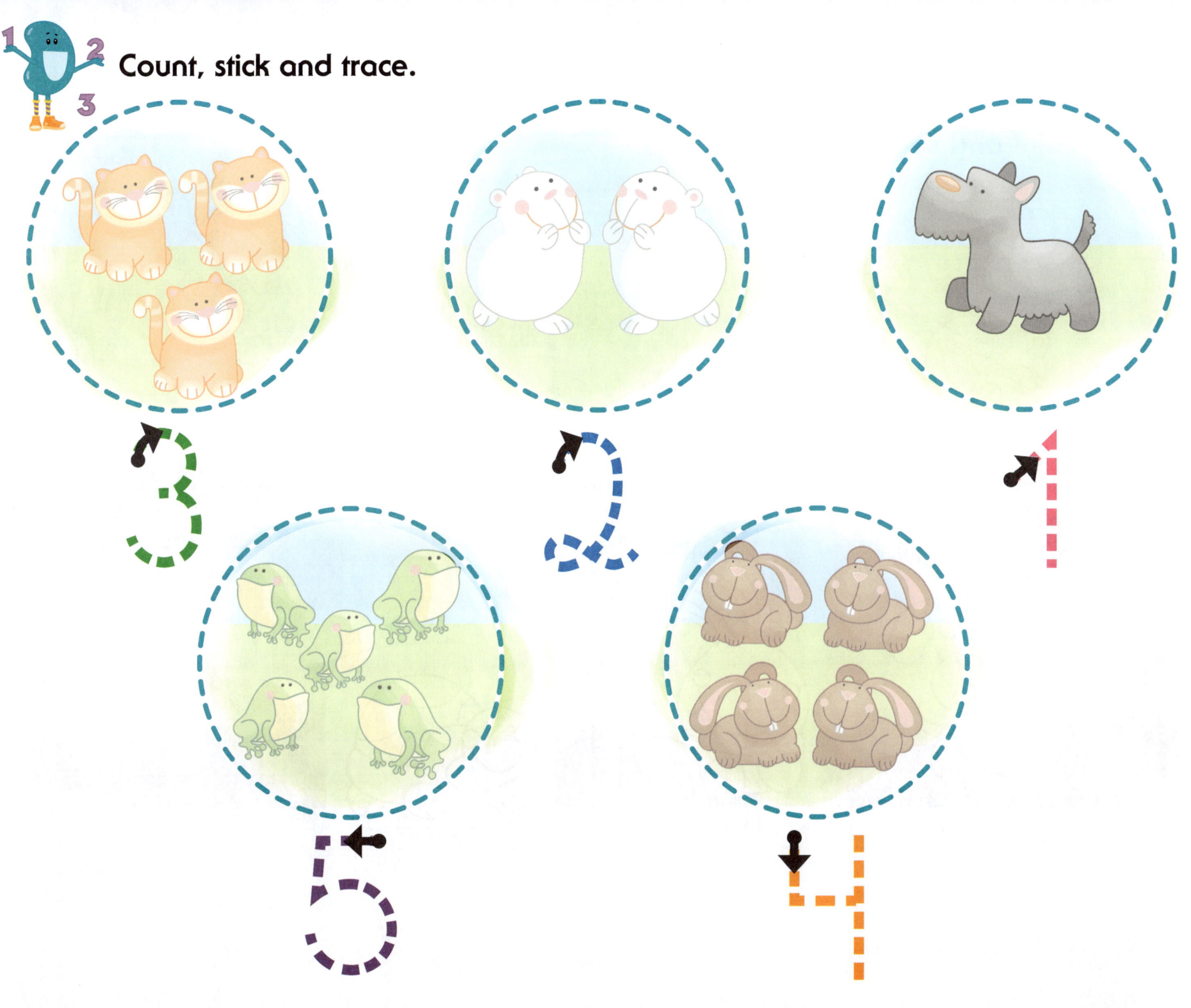

Point and color.

38 Unit 6 **Pets** Review

Unit 7
Toys

Point, color and trace.

Unit 7 Toys   Lesson 1

Point and color.

Unit 7 Toys Lesson 1

Look and stick.

42 — Unit 7 **Toys** Lesson 2

Point and stick.

Unit 7 **Toys** Lesson 2

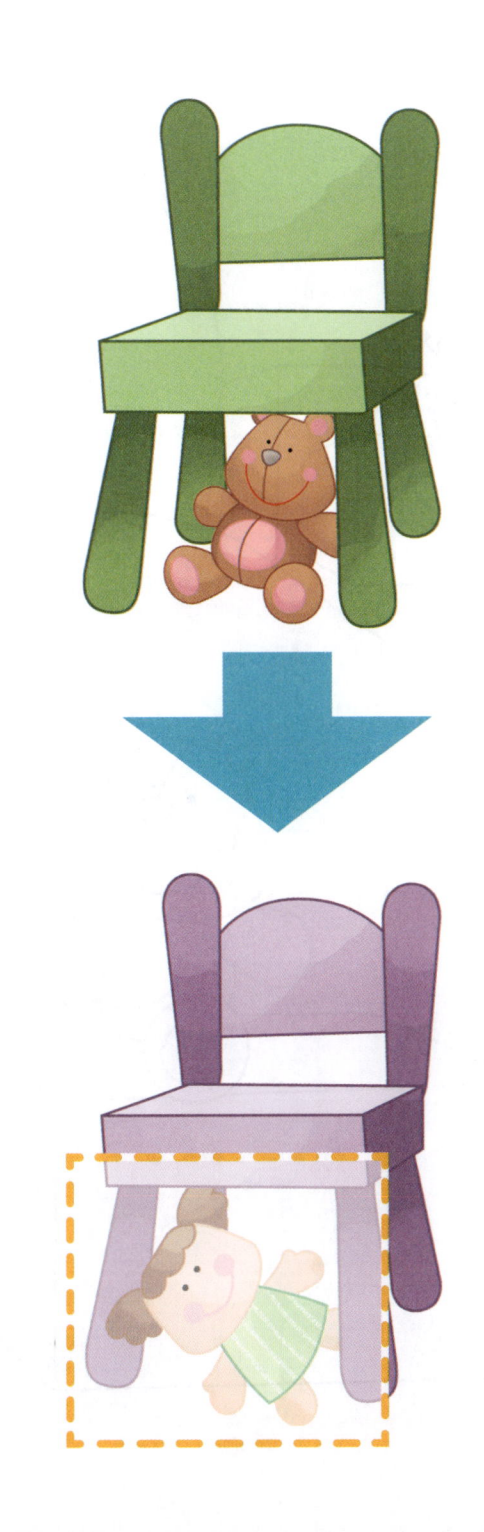

Look and color.

Unit 8
Food

Point and color.

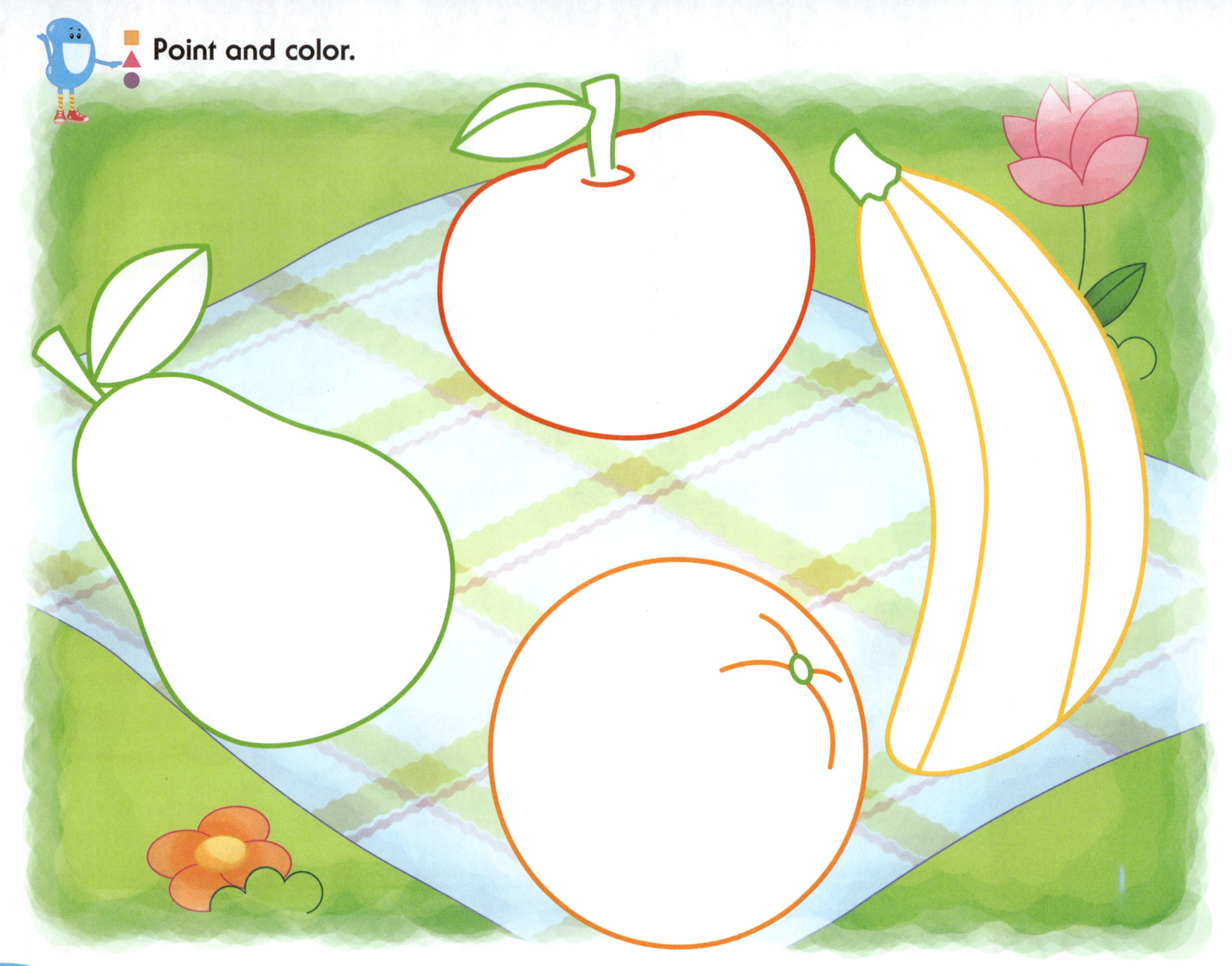

46 Unit 8 Food Lesson 1

Trace and color.

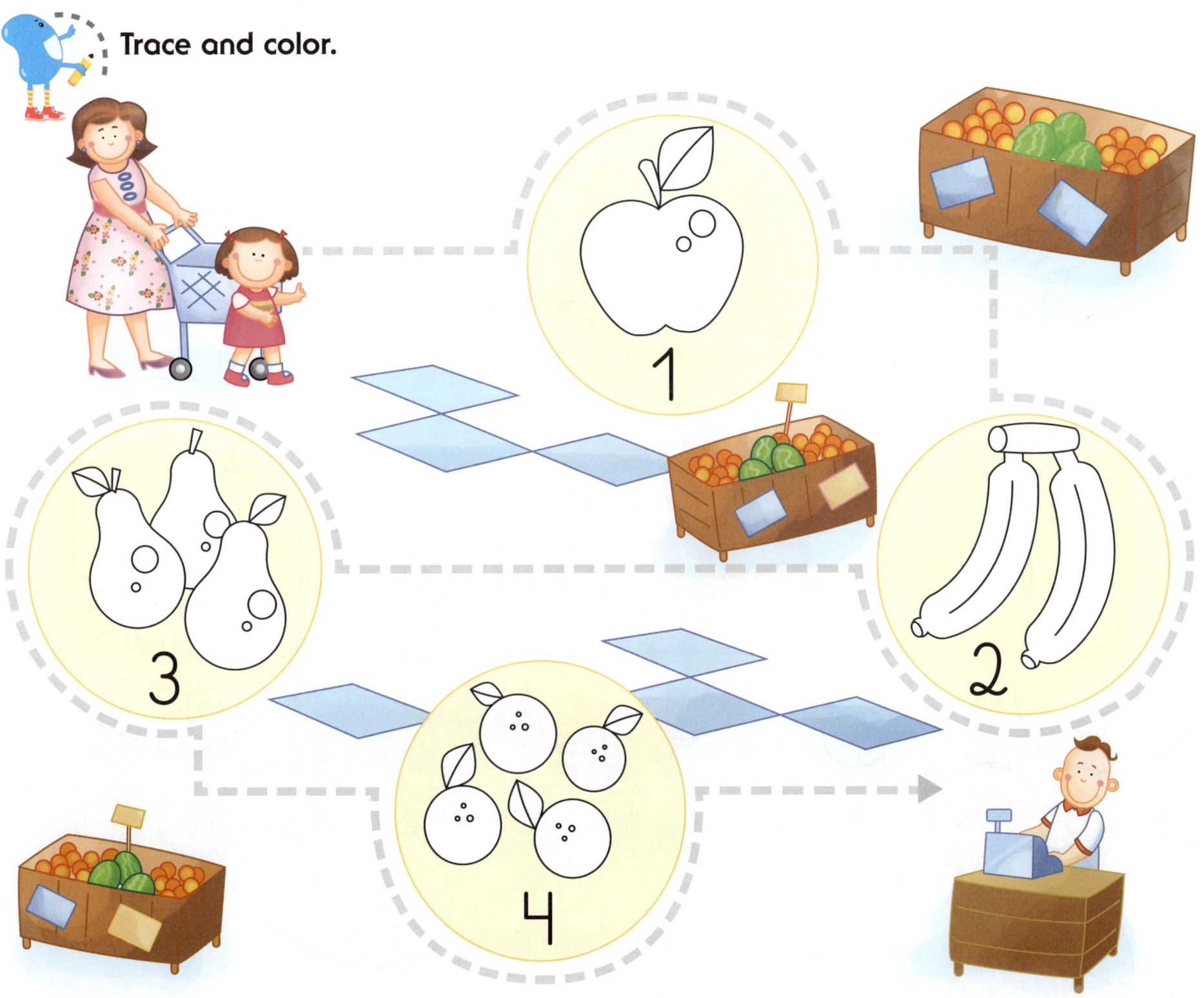

1
2
3
4

Jellybeans 1

Unit 8 Food   Lesson 1

47

Point, color and match.

Unit 8 Food   Lesson 2

Point and stick.

Unit 8 Food   Lesson 2

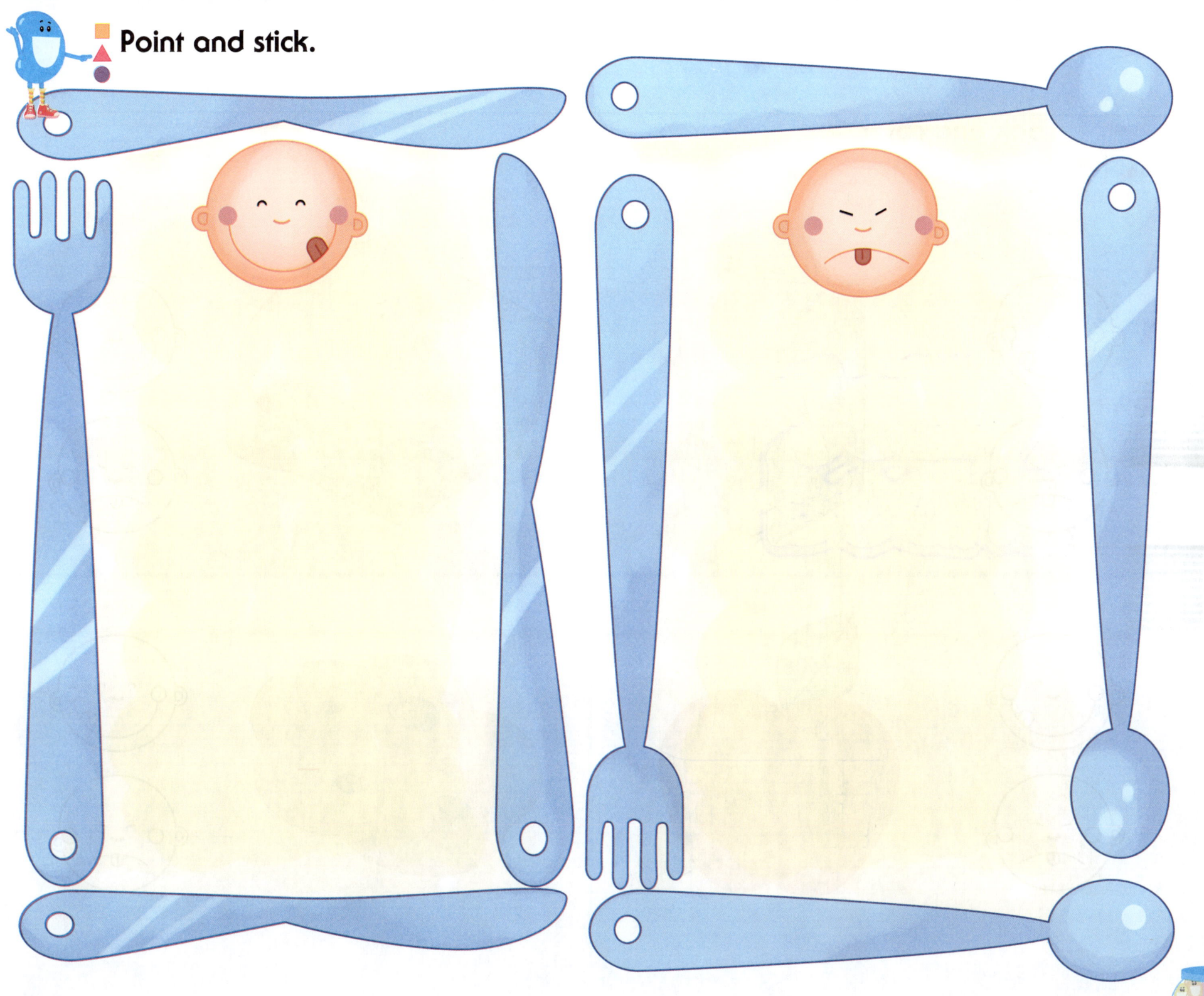

Look and color.

50 Unit 8 **Food** Review

Unit 1 I go to school

- crayon
- book
- table
- lunch box
- pencil
- chair

Unit 2 Colors and numbers

- circle
- 1 one
- triangle
- 2 two
- square
- 3 three

Jellybeans 1

Picture dictionary   51

Unit 3 My face

- hair
- eyes
- ears
- mouth
- nose

Unit 4 My family

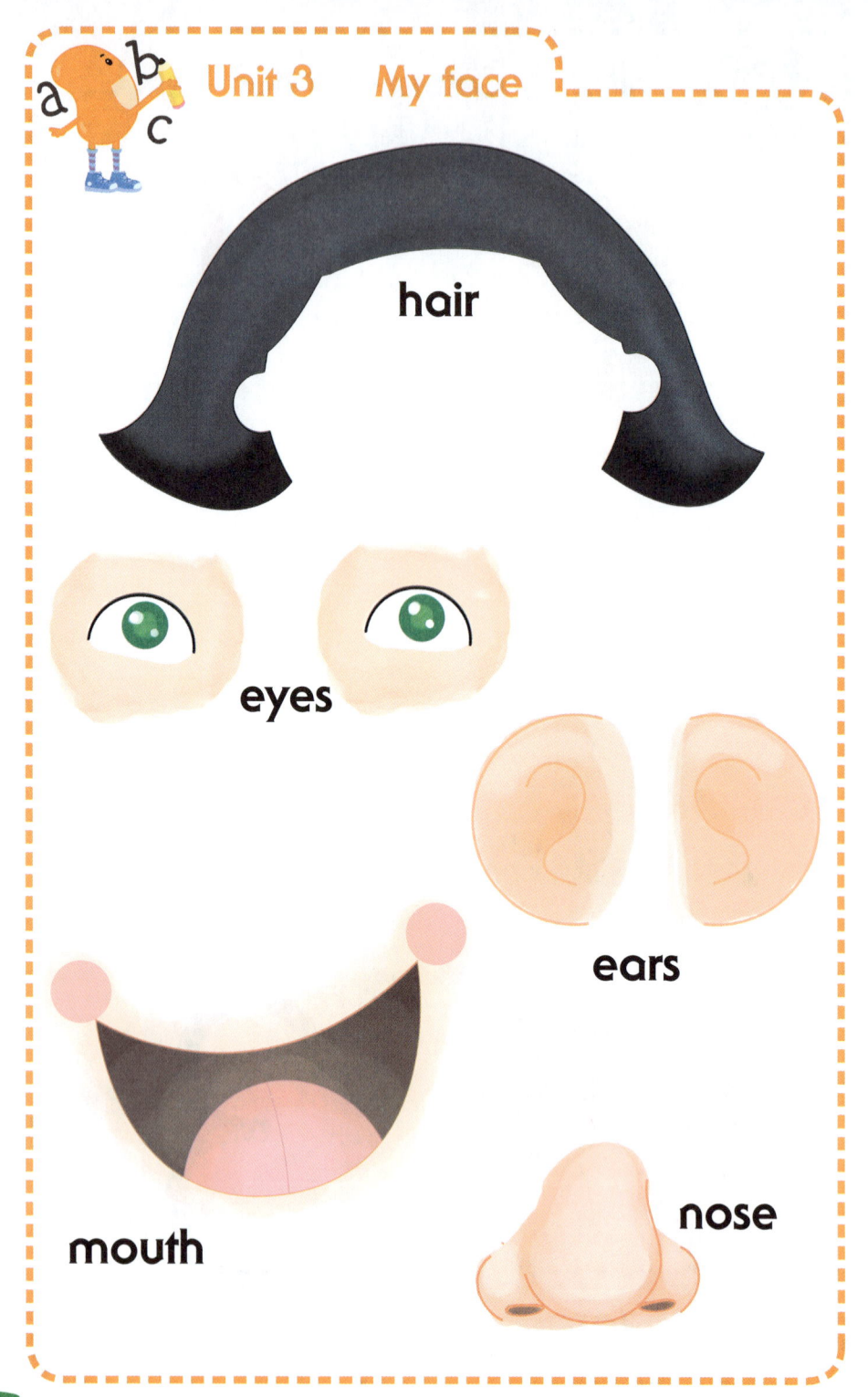

- baby
- sister
- grandpa
- grandma
- mommy
- brother
- daddy

52 Picture dictionary

Jellybeans 1

Unit 5 Nature

bird

flower

tree

butterfly

park

Unit 6 Pets

dog

hamster

fish

turtle

frog

cat

rabbit

Picture dictionary

Unit 7 Toys

- ball
- car
- teddy bear
- doll
- toy box

Unit 8 Food

- sandwich
- orange
- apple
- banana
- cookie
- carrot
- pear

Picture dictionary

Jellybean awards this certificate to

_____

(NAME) _____

for completing

Jelly beans

CONGRATULATIONS!

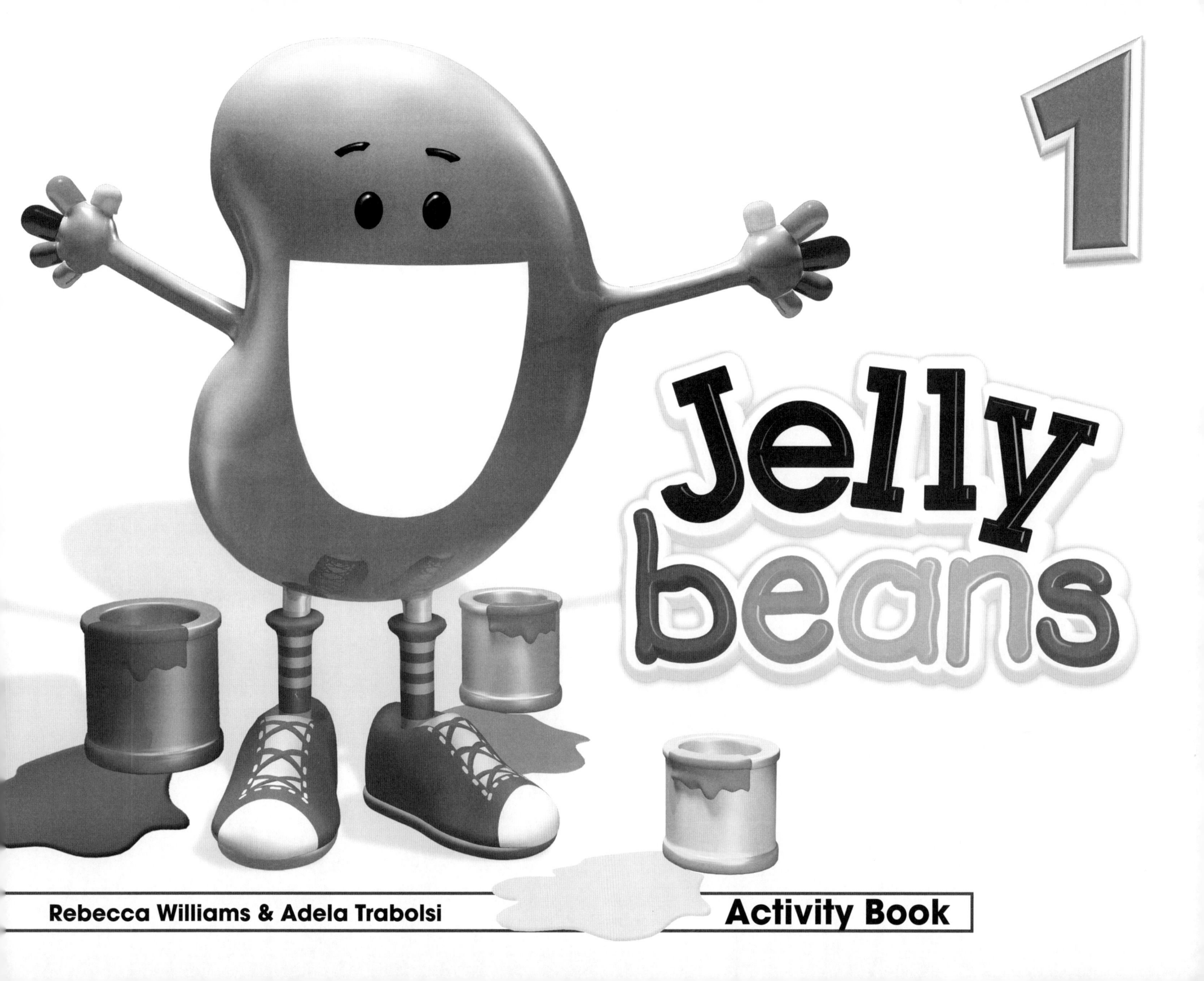

Jelly beans

1

Rebecca Williams & Adela Trabolsi

Activity Book

Cut, glue and color.

Boys

Girls

Jellybeans 1

Unit 1   **I go to school**   Lesson 1

60   Unit 1   **I go to school**   Lesson 1

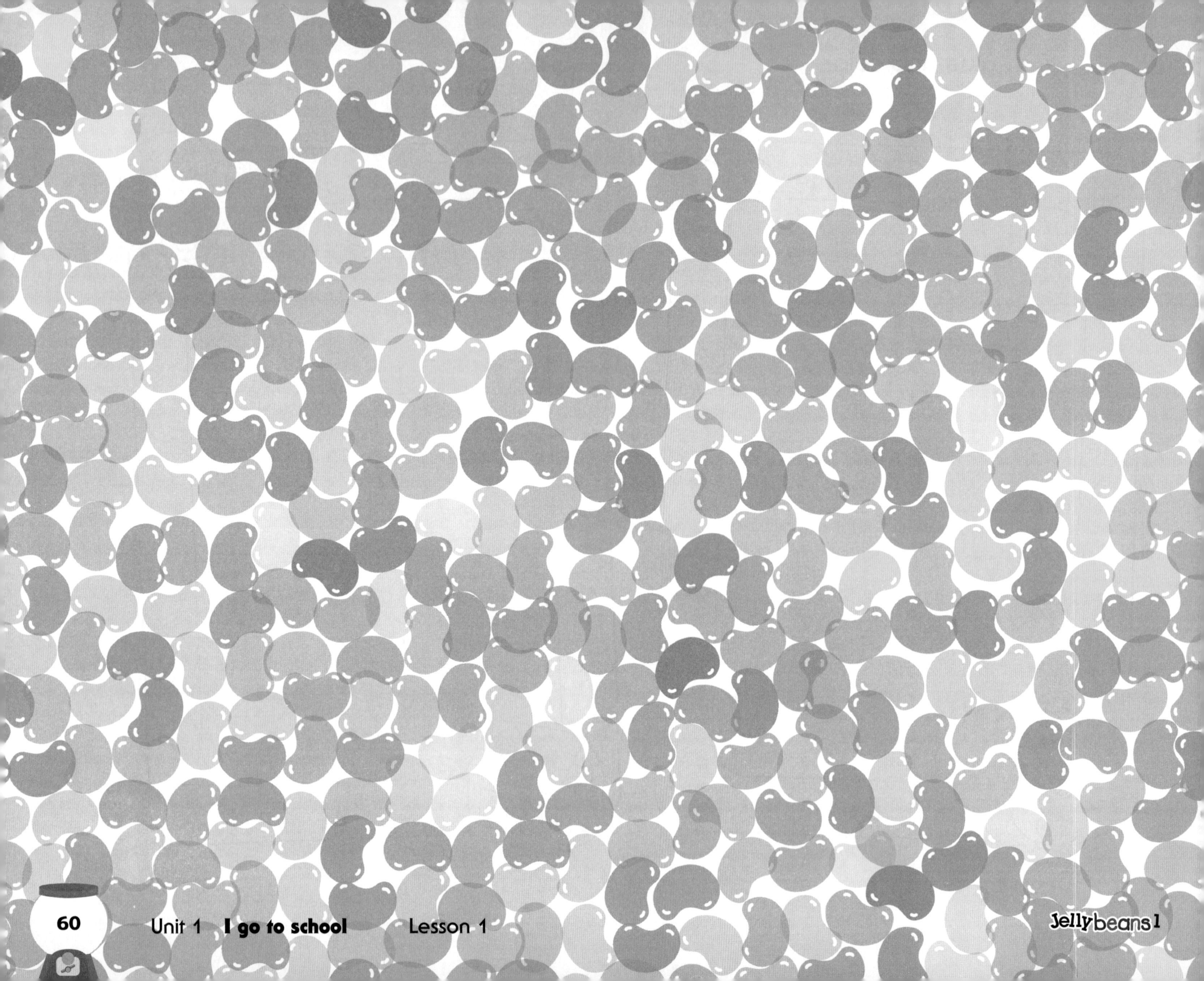

Color, cut and glue.

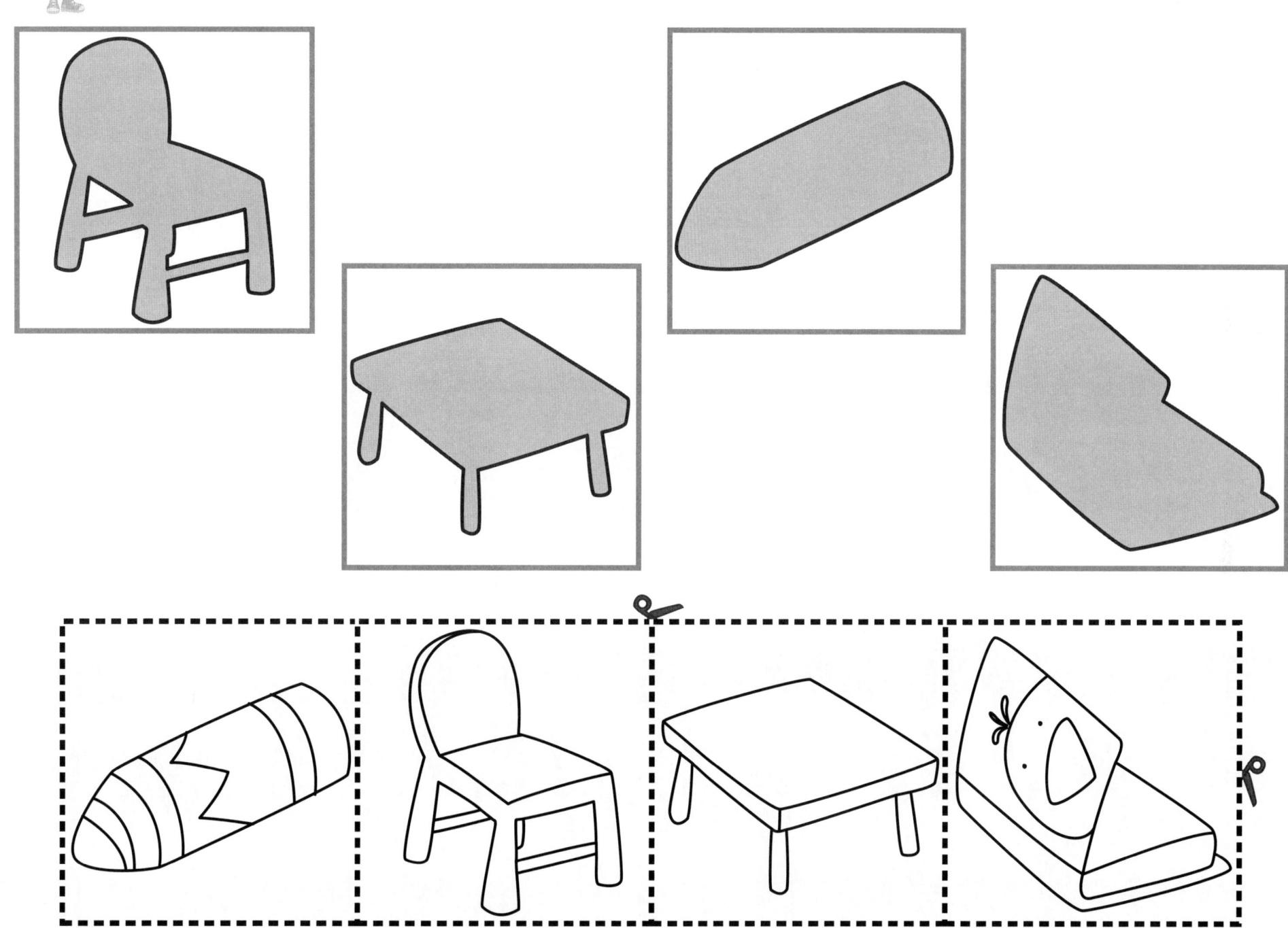

Unit 1 **I go to school** Lesson 1

62　　Unit 1　**I go to school**　　Lesson 1

Jellybeans 1

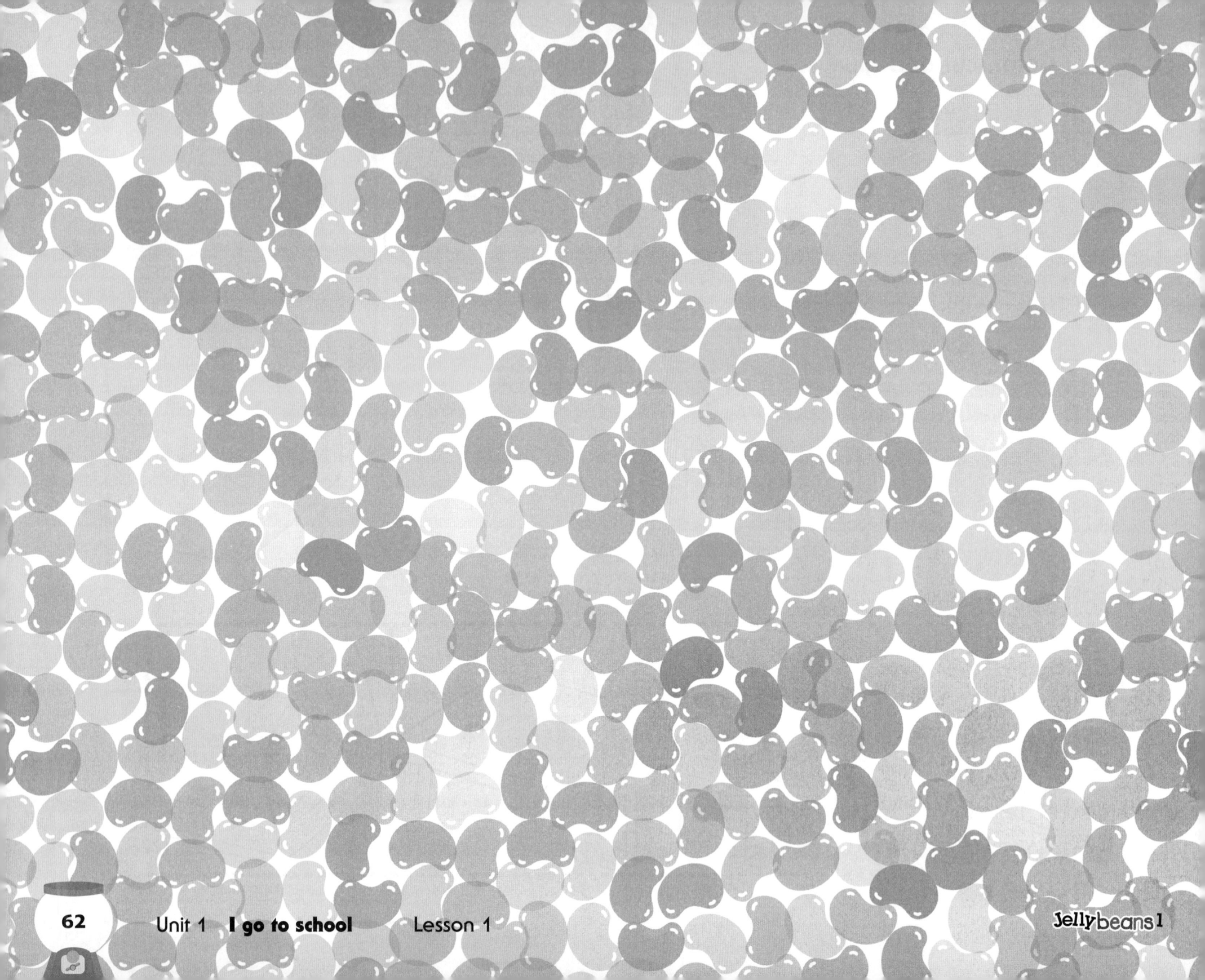

Color, cut and play *Concentration*.

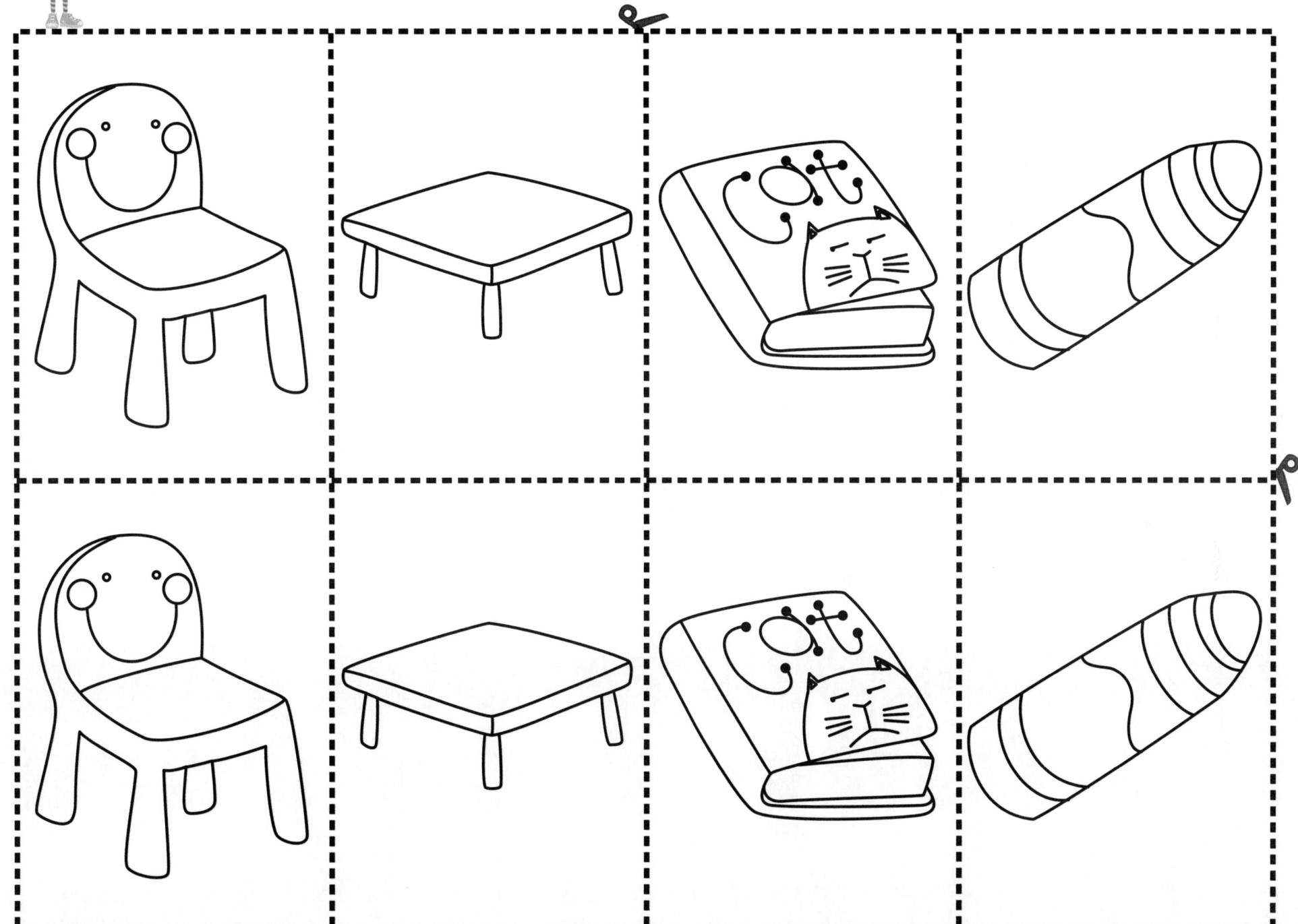

Unit 1   **I go to school**   Lesson 2

64 Unit 1 **I go to school** Lesson 2

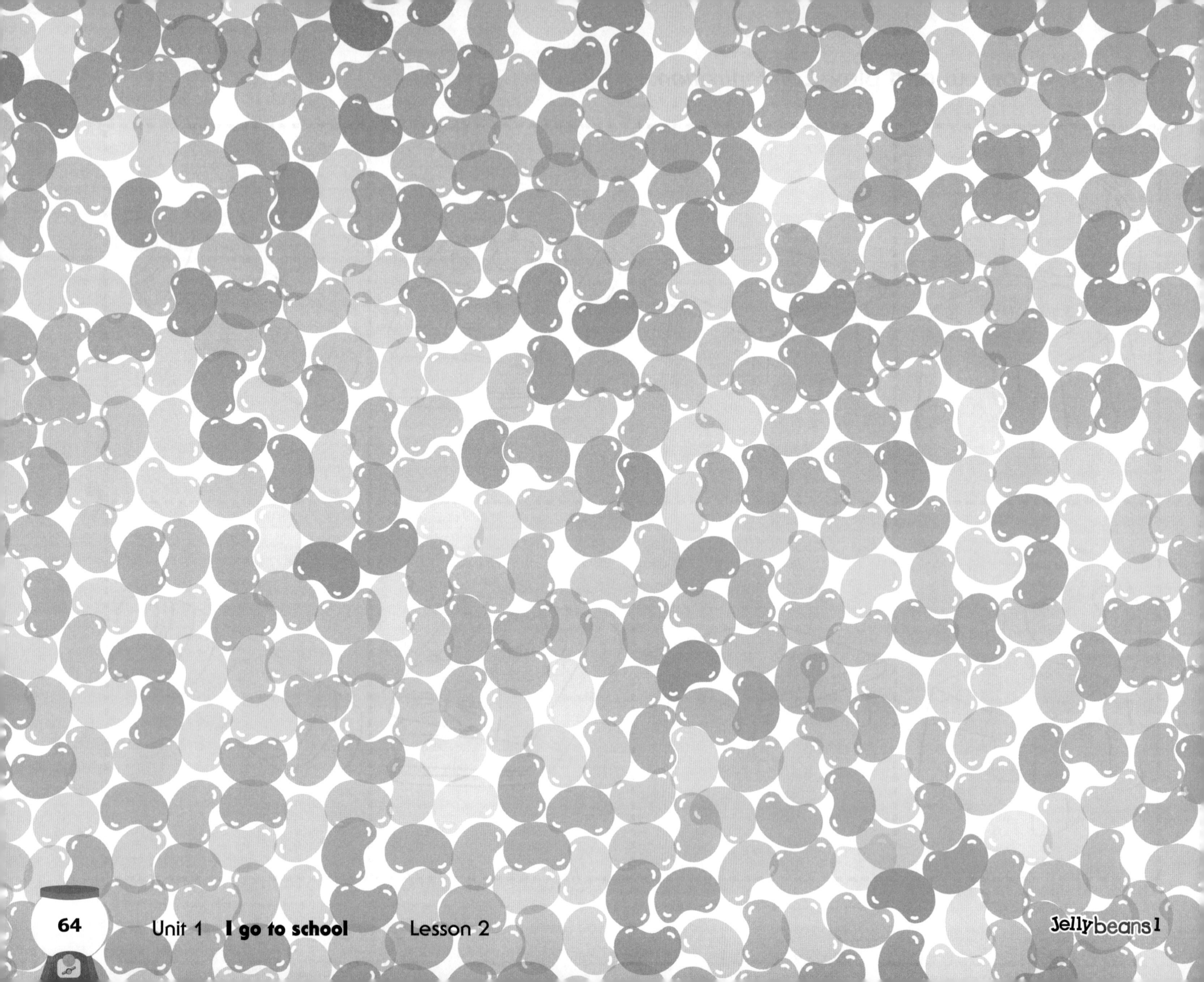

Trace, color and glue.

Jellybeans 1   Unit 1   **I go to school**   Lesson 2   65

66 Unit 1 **I go to school** Lesson 2

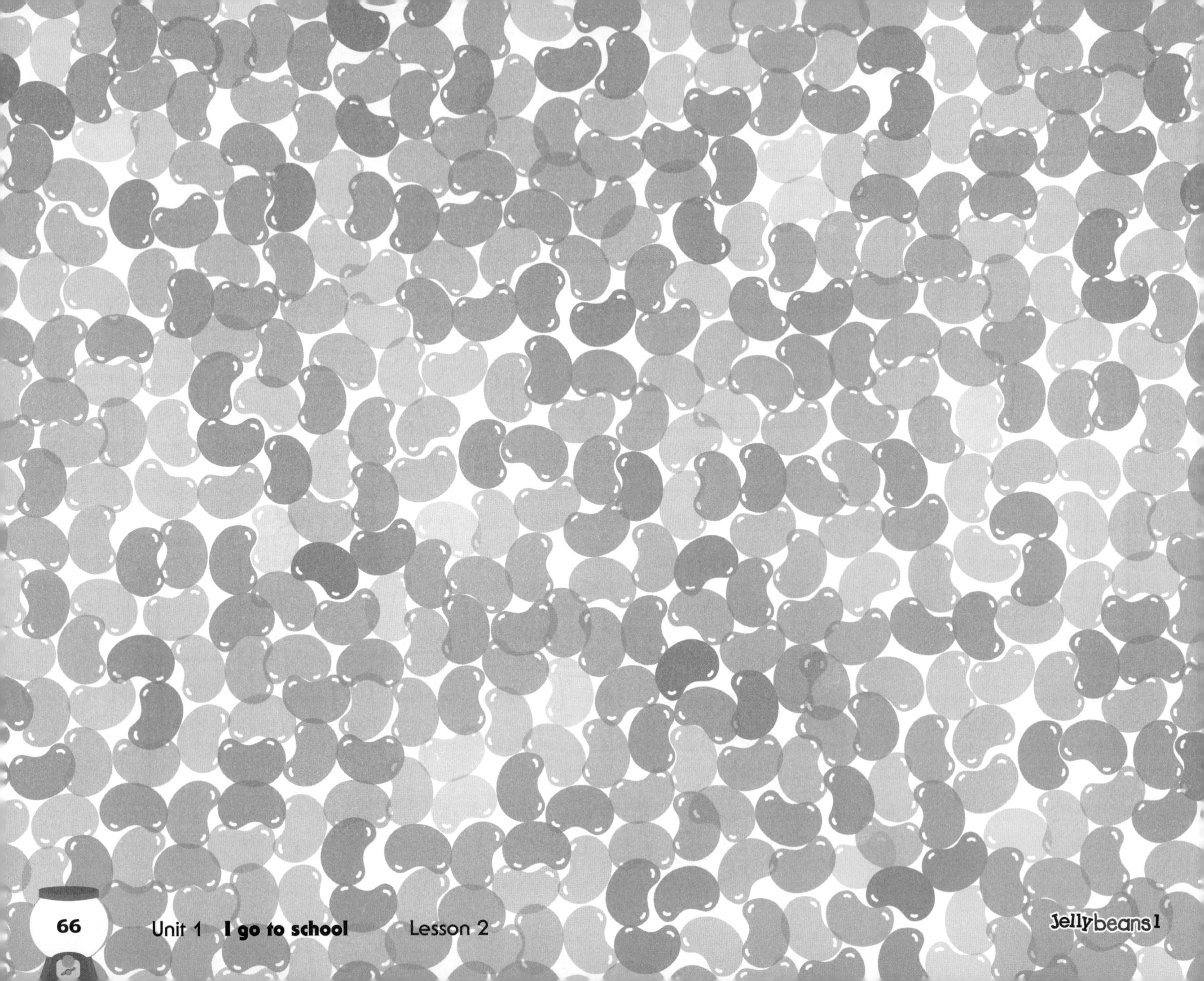

Look and glue.

Jellybeans 1 — Unit 2 **Colors and numbers** — Lesson 1 — 67

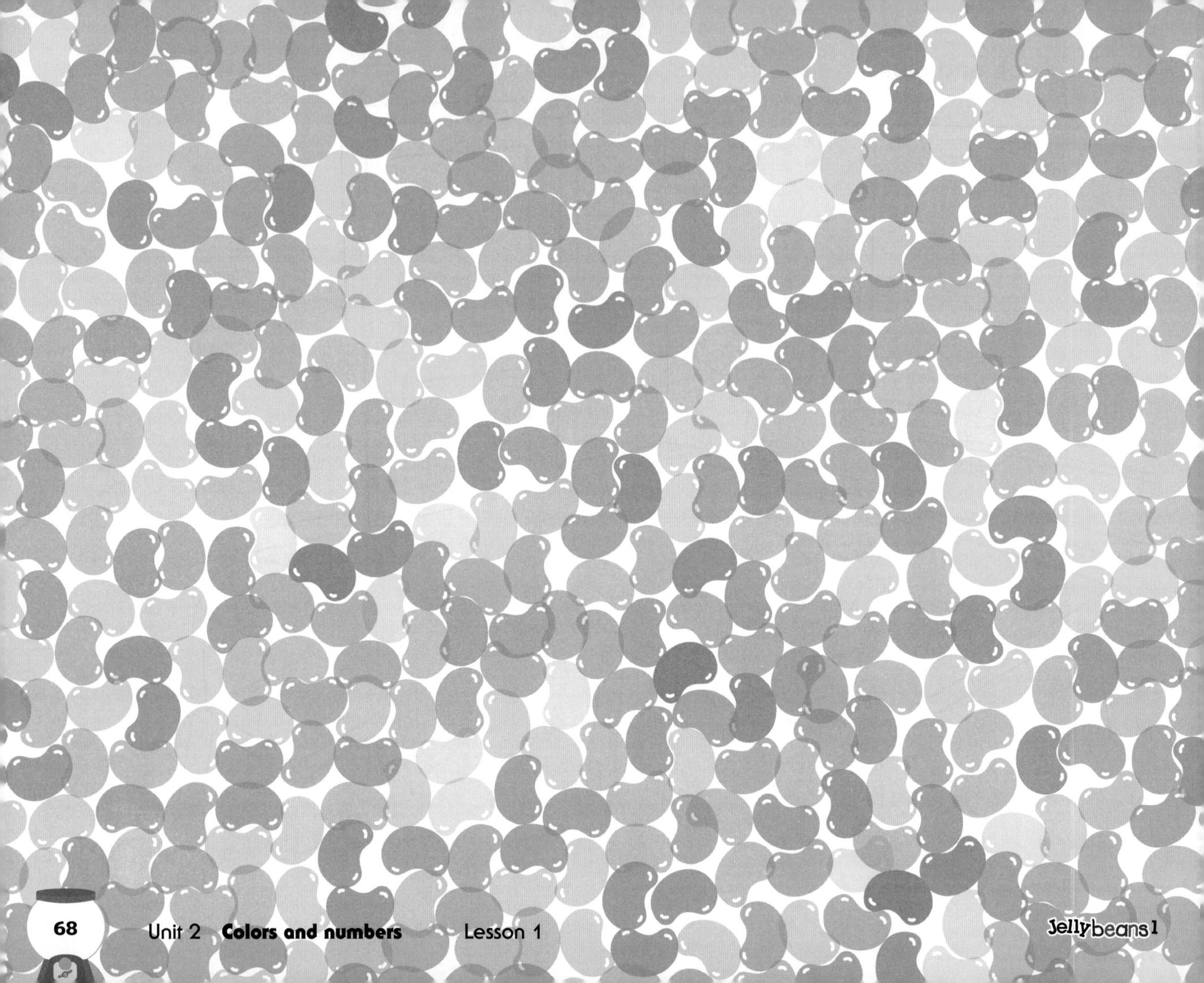

Color and cut.

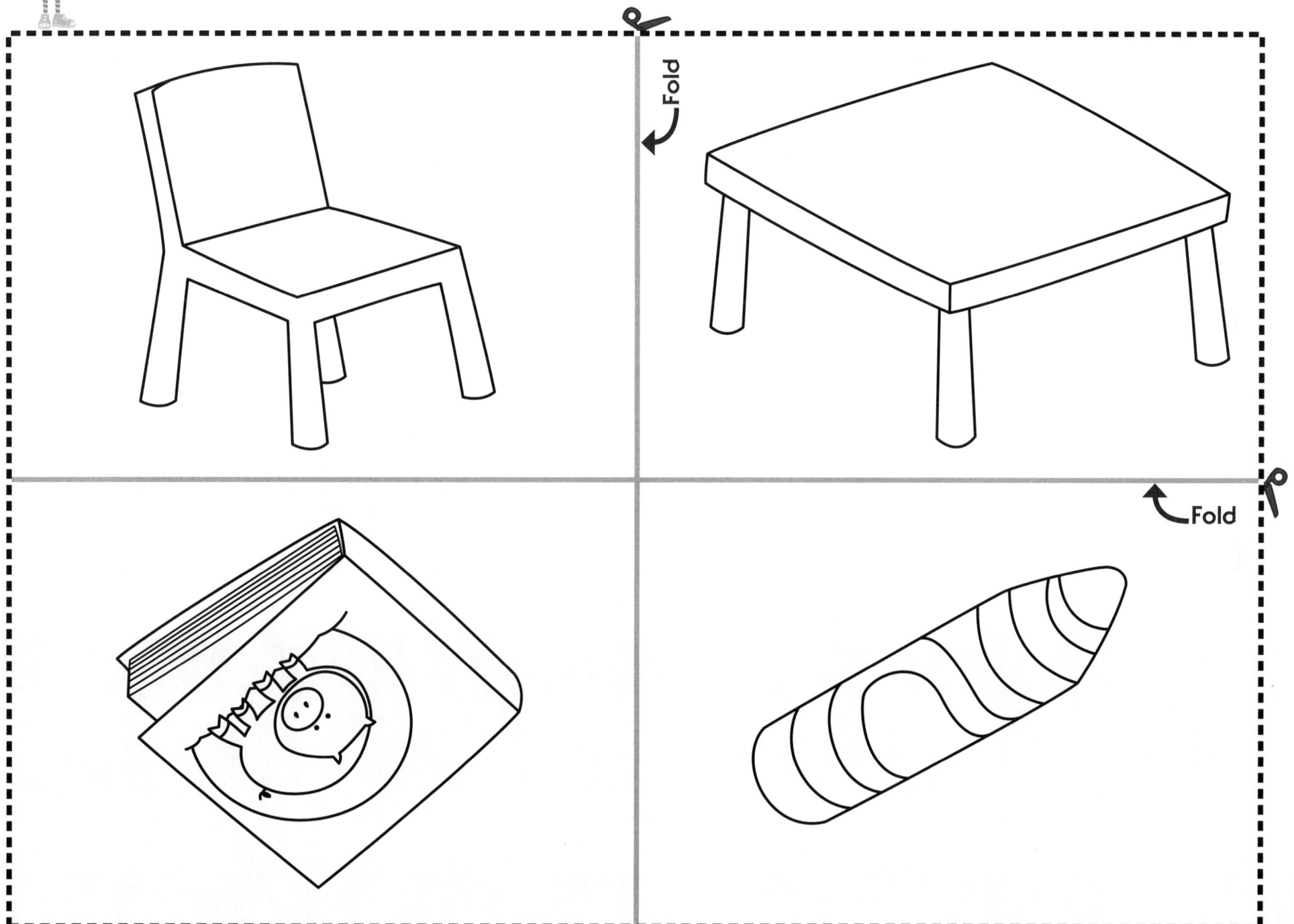

Fold

Fold

Jellybeans 1 — Unit 2 **Colors and numbers** — Lesson 1 — 69

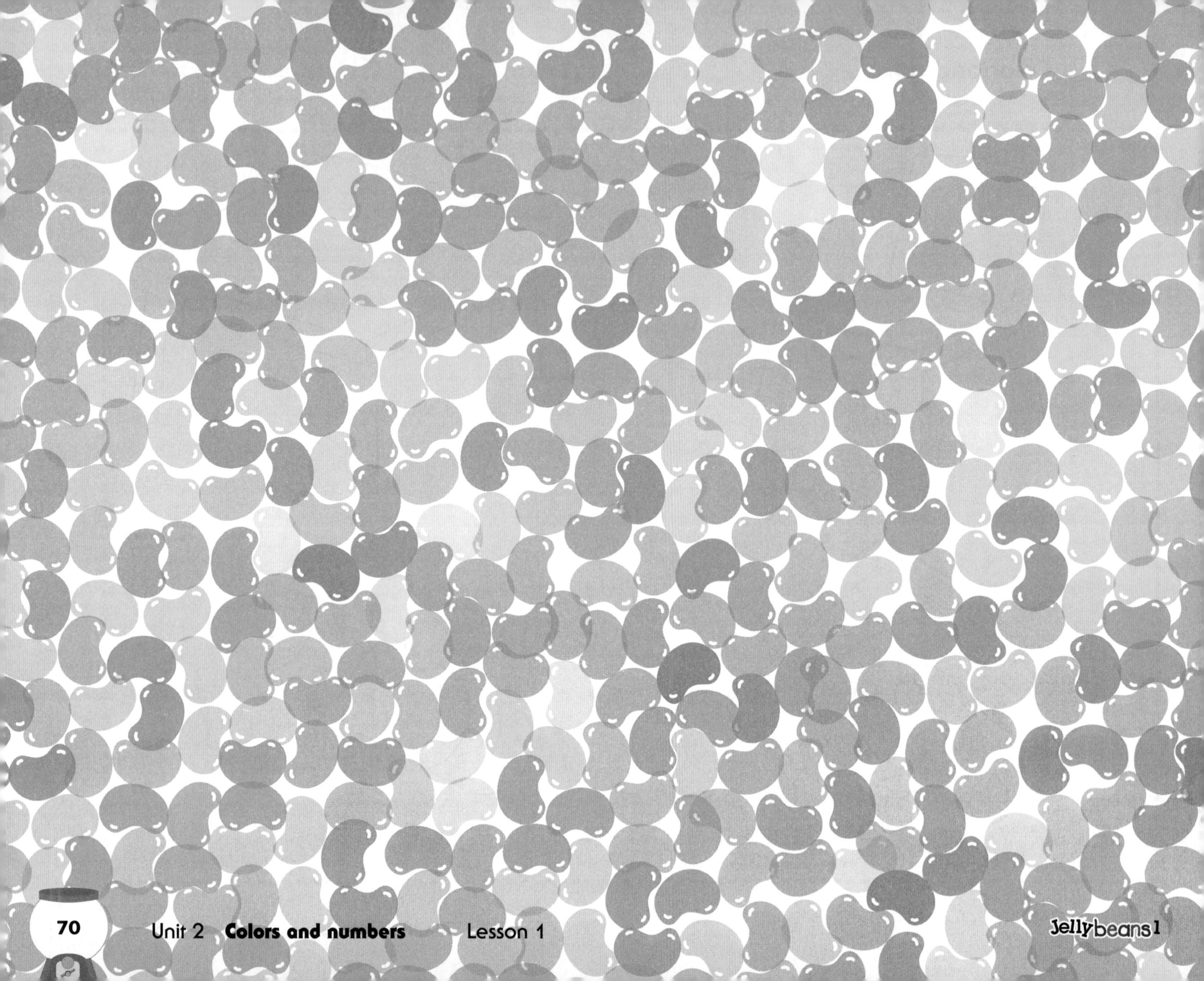

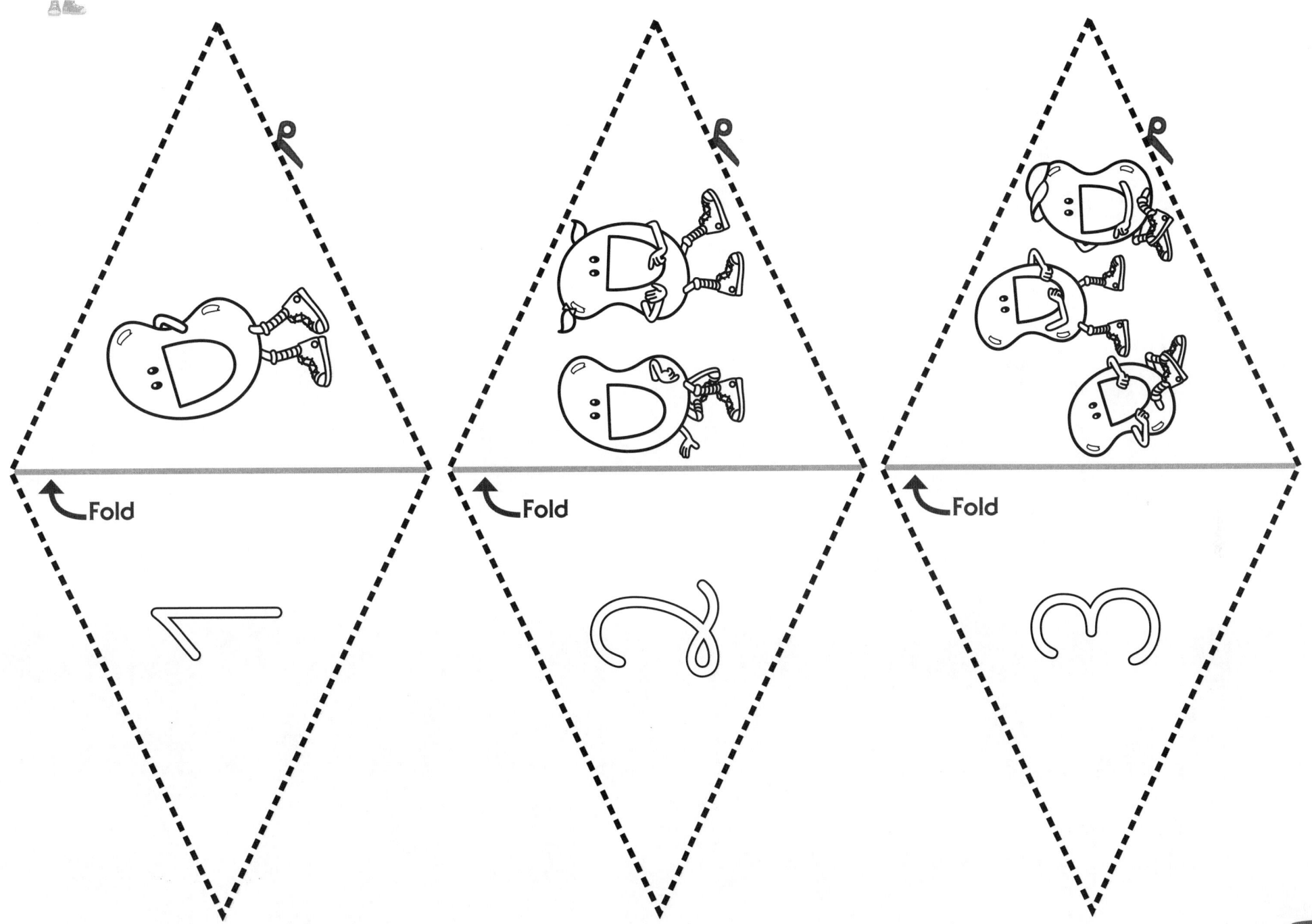

Color, cut and glue.

Fold

Fold

Fold

Jellybeans 1 · Unit 2 **Colors and numbers** · Lesson 2

72 Unit 2 **Colors and numbers** Lesson 2

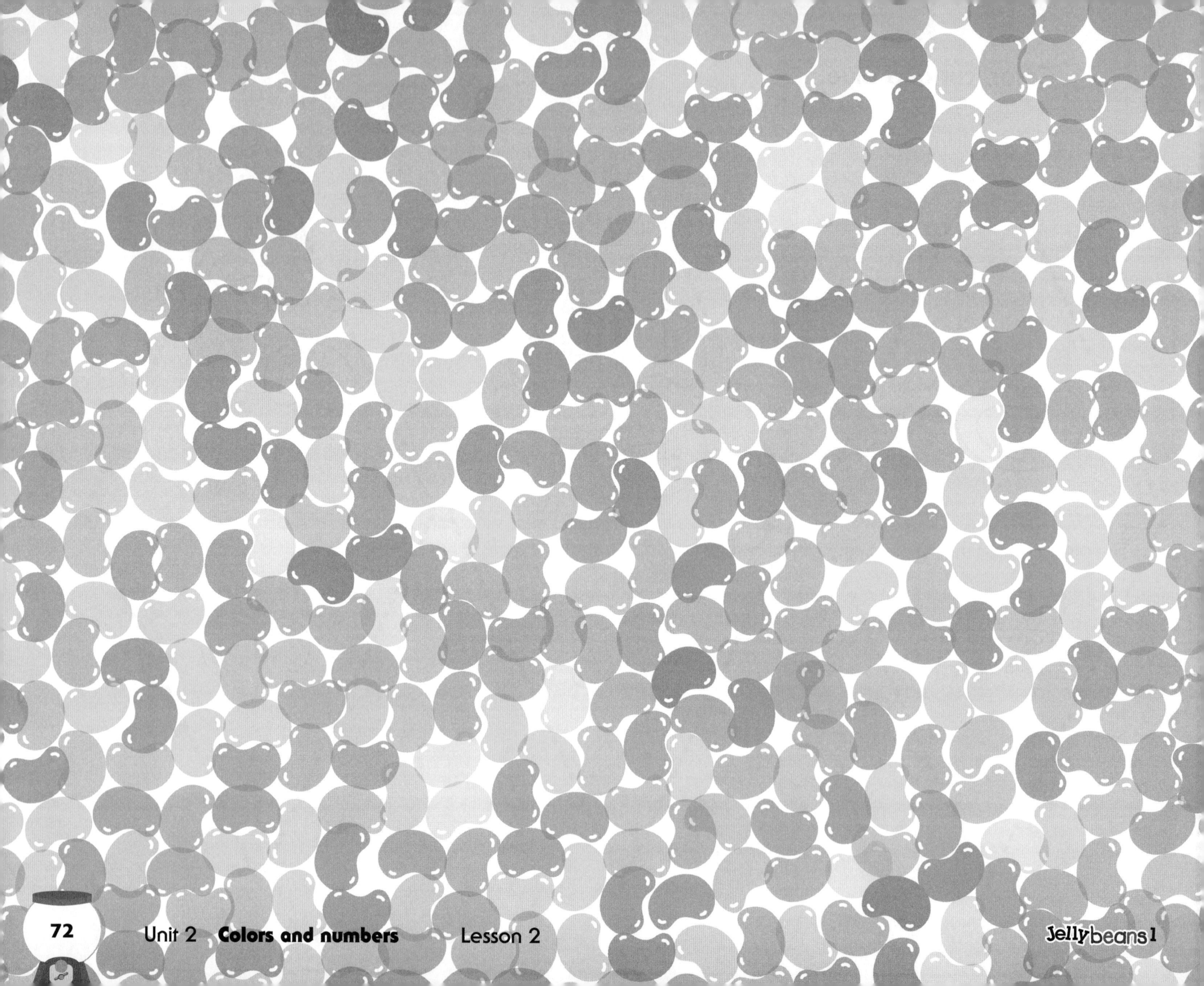

Count, trace and color.

Unit 2 **Colors and numbers** Lesson 2

74 Unit 2 **Colors and numbers** Lesson 2

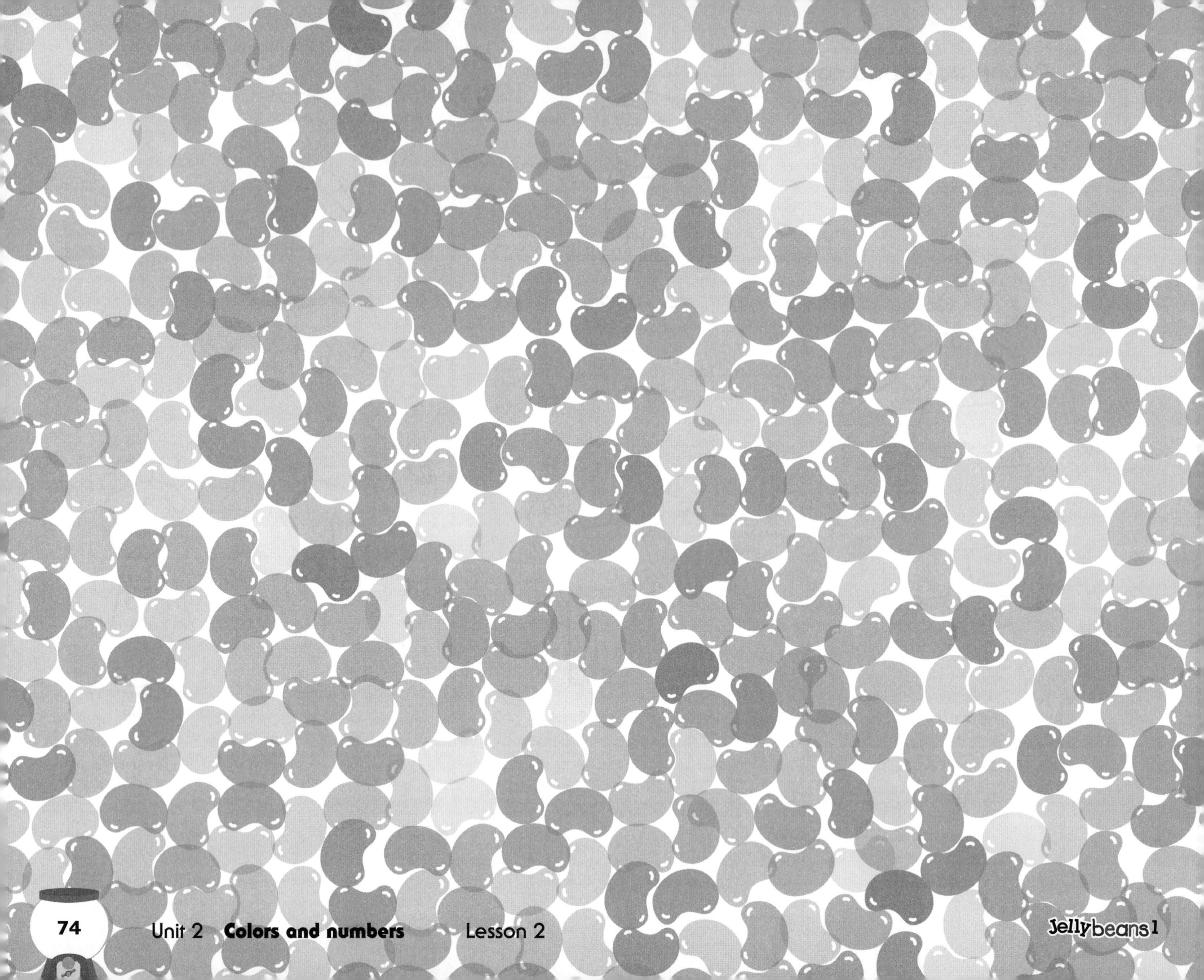

Trace, glue and color.

Jellybeans 1 Unit 3 **My face** Lesson 1 75

Unit 3 **My face** Lesson 1

Jellybeans 1

Cut and paint.

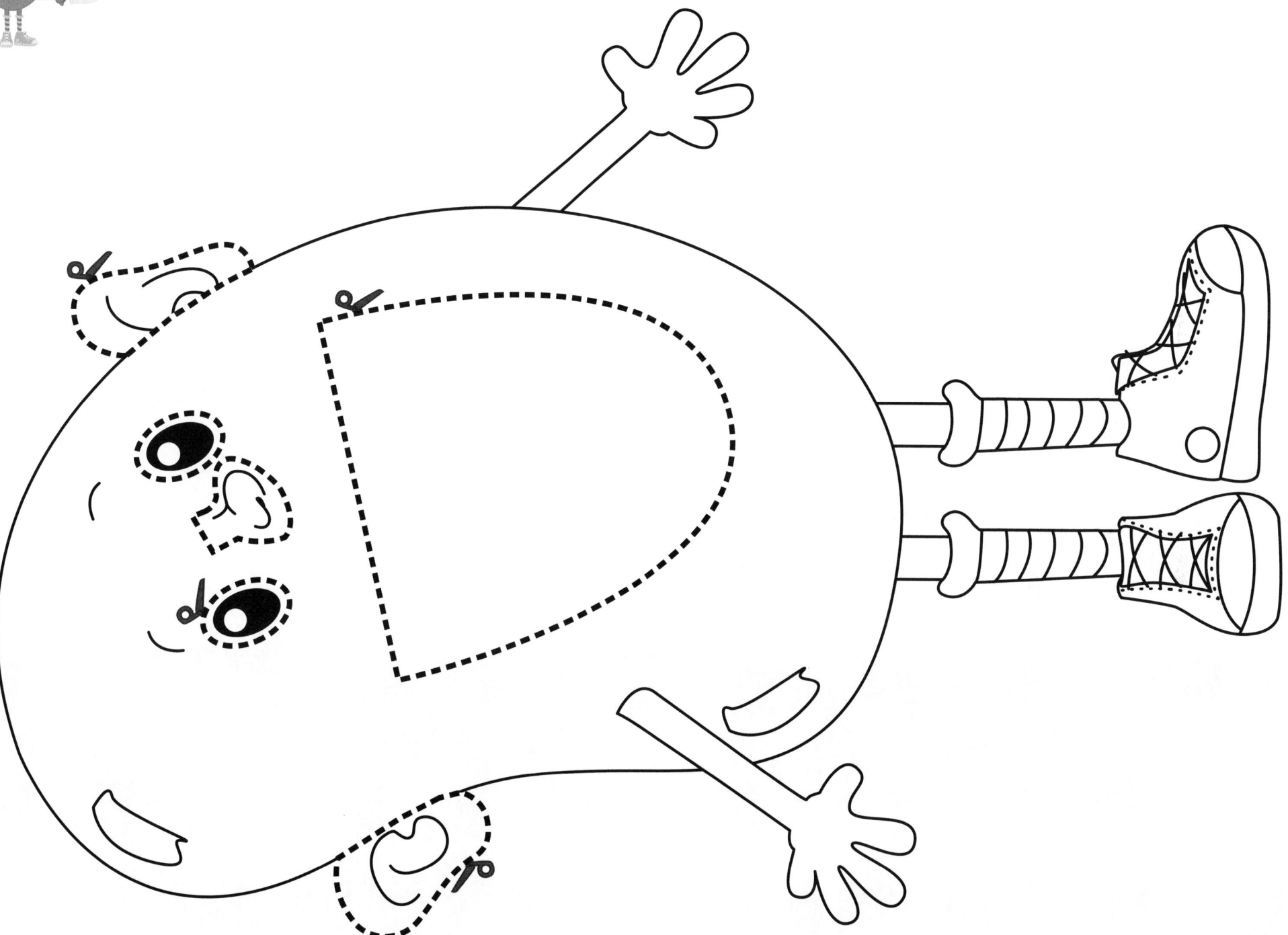

Jellybeans 1   Unit 3   **My face**   Lesson 1   77

78   Unit 3   **My face**   Lesson 1

Cut and glue.

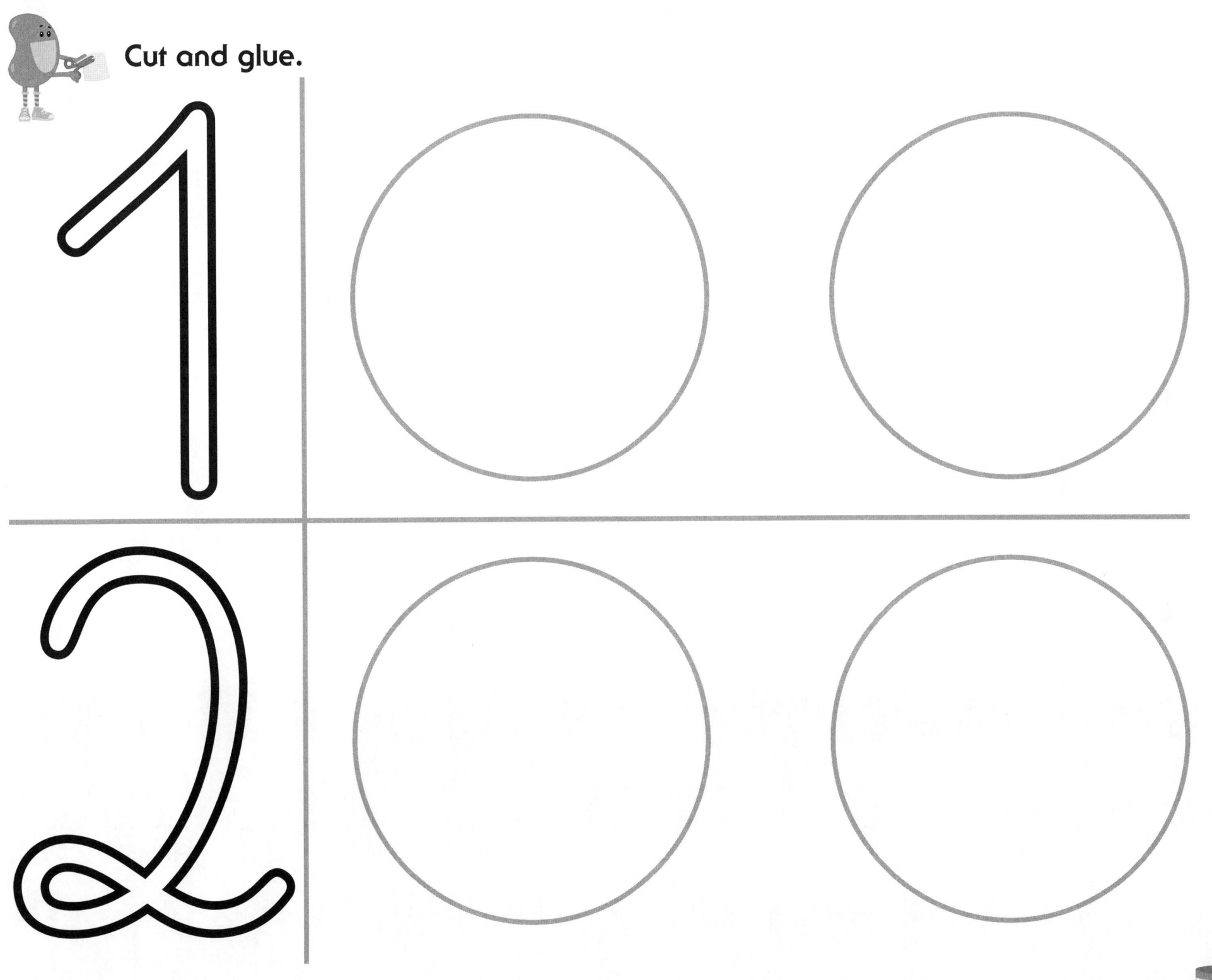

1

2

Jellybeans 1

Unit 3 **My face** Lesson 2

79

80　　Unit 3　**My face**　　Lesson 2

Match and glue.

Jellybeans 1

Unit 3 **My face** Lesson 2

81

82   Unit 3   **My face**   Lesson 2

Color, cut and glue.

Unit 4 **My family** Lesson 1

84 Unit 4 **My family** Lesson 1

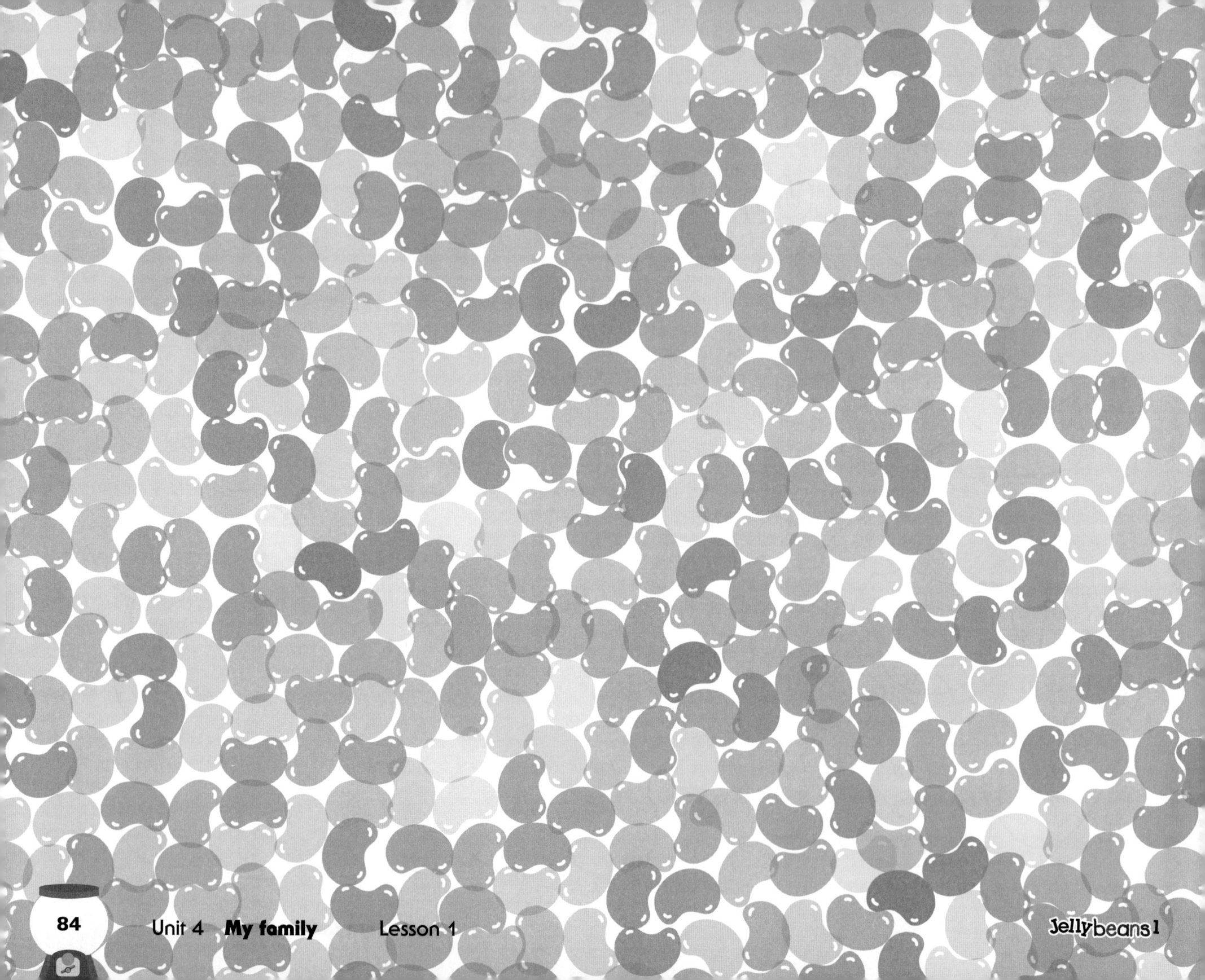

Jellybeans 1

Color, finger-paint, cut and glue.

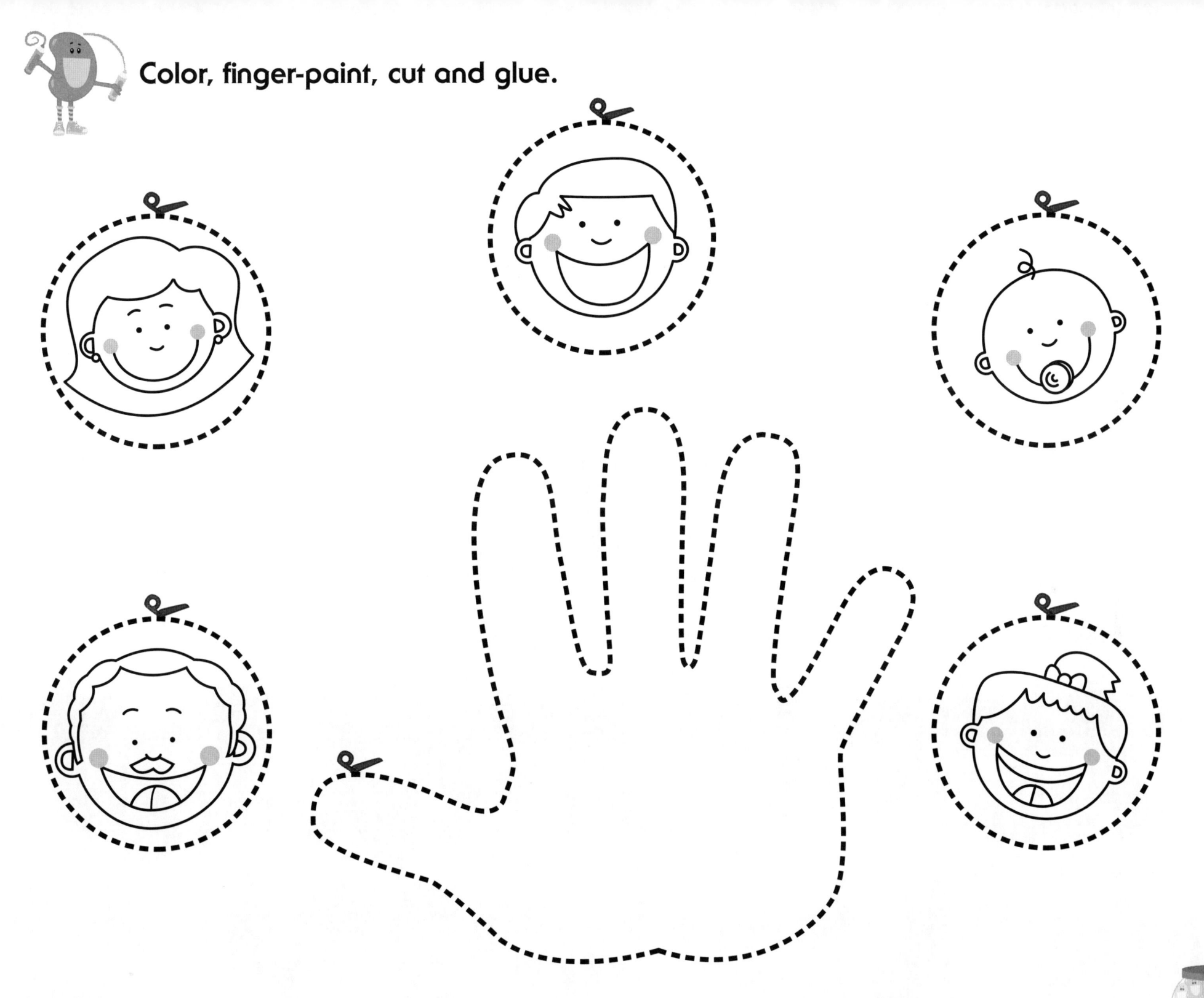

Jellybeans 1

Unit 4 **My family** Lesson 1

85

86 Unit 4 **My family** Lesson 1

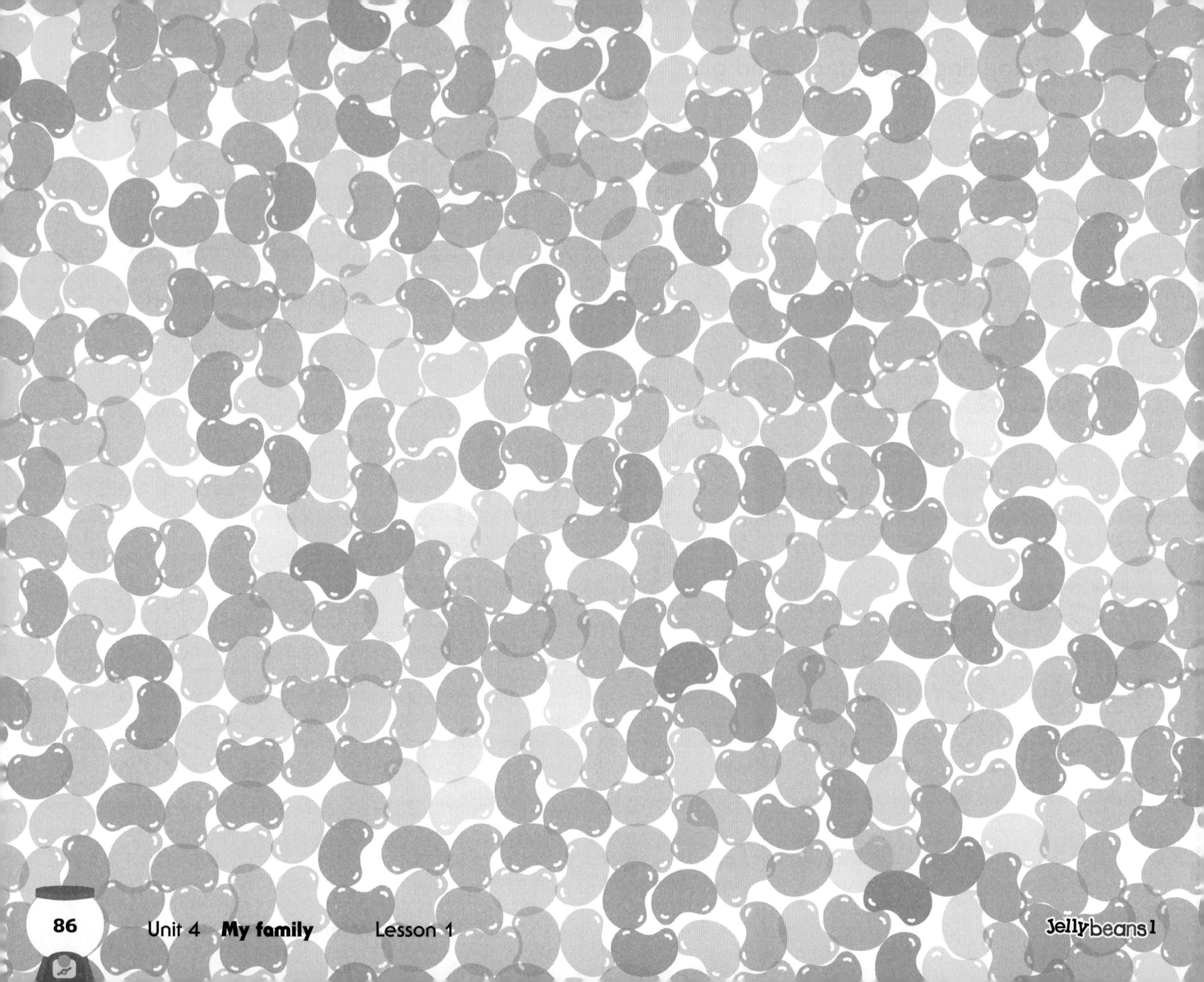

Color, cut and glue.

Jellybeans 1

Unit 4 **My family** Lesson 2

87

88 Unit 4 **My family** Lesson 2

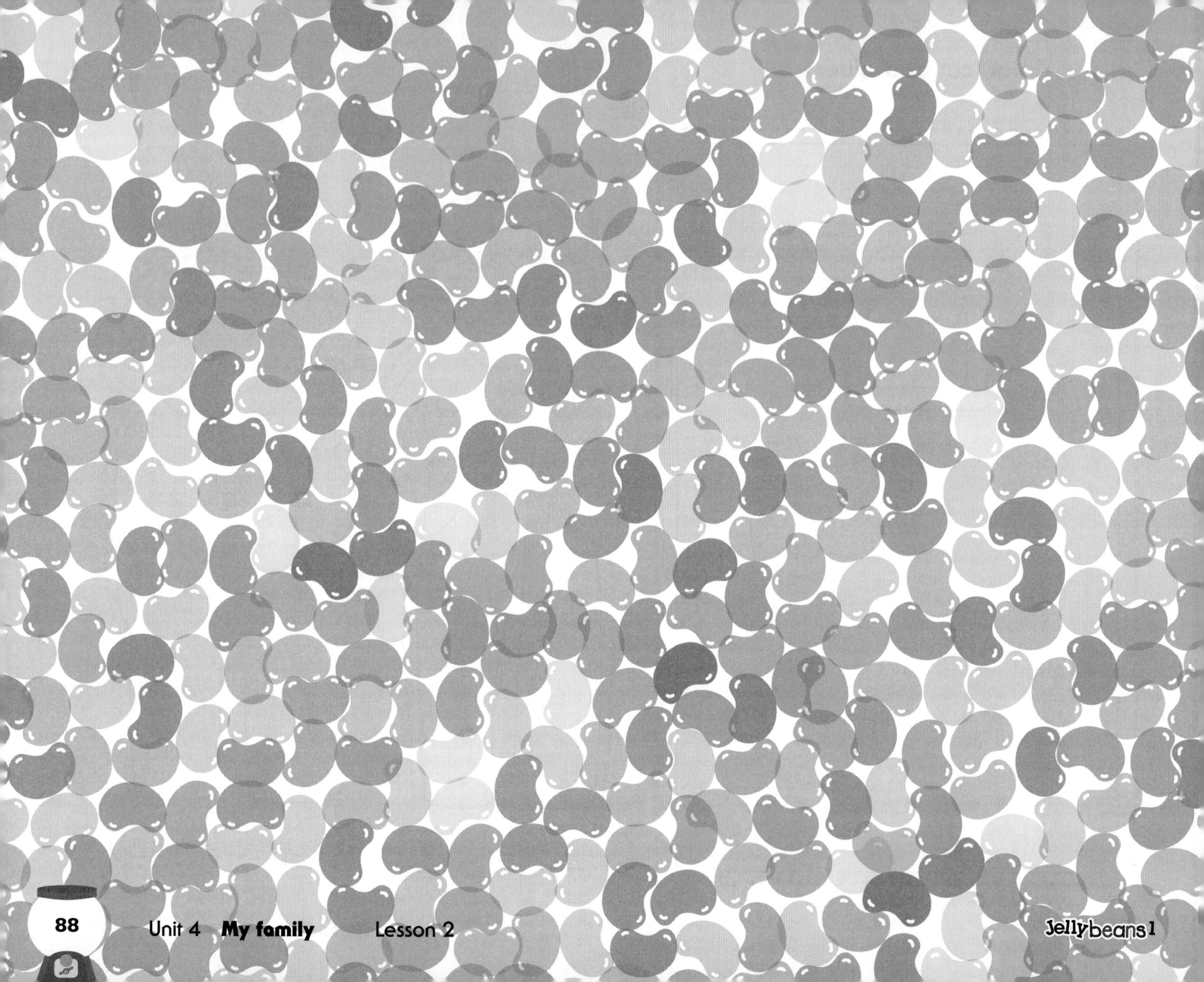

Color, cut and glue.

Unit 4   **My family**   Lesson 2

Unit 4 **My family** Lesson 2

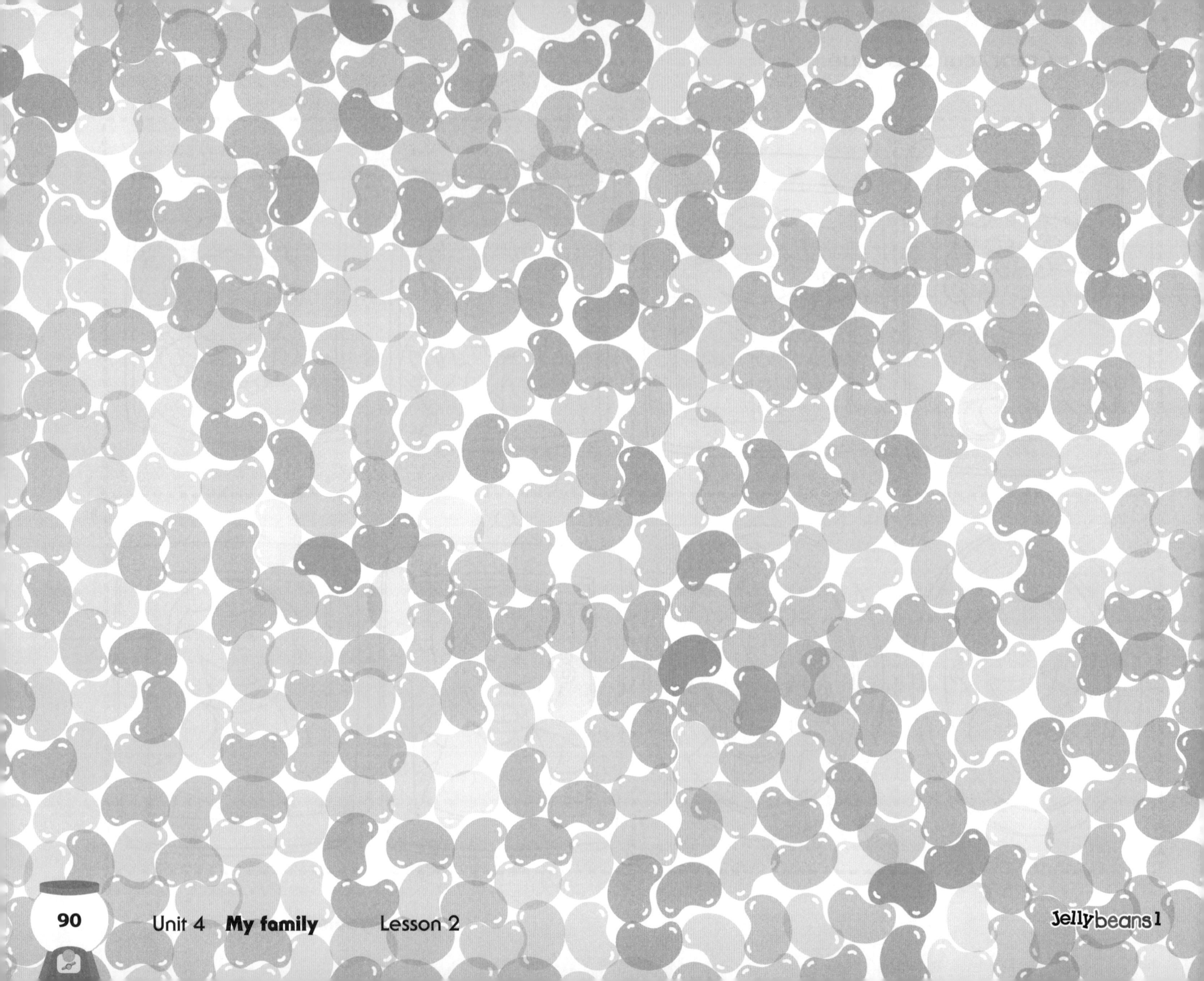

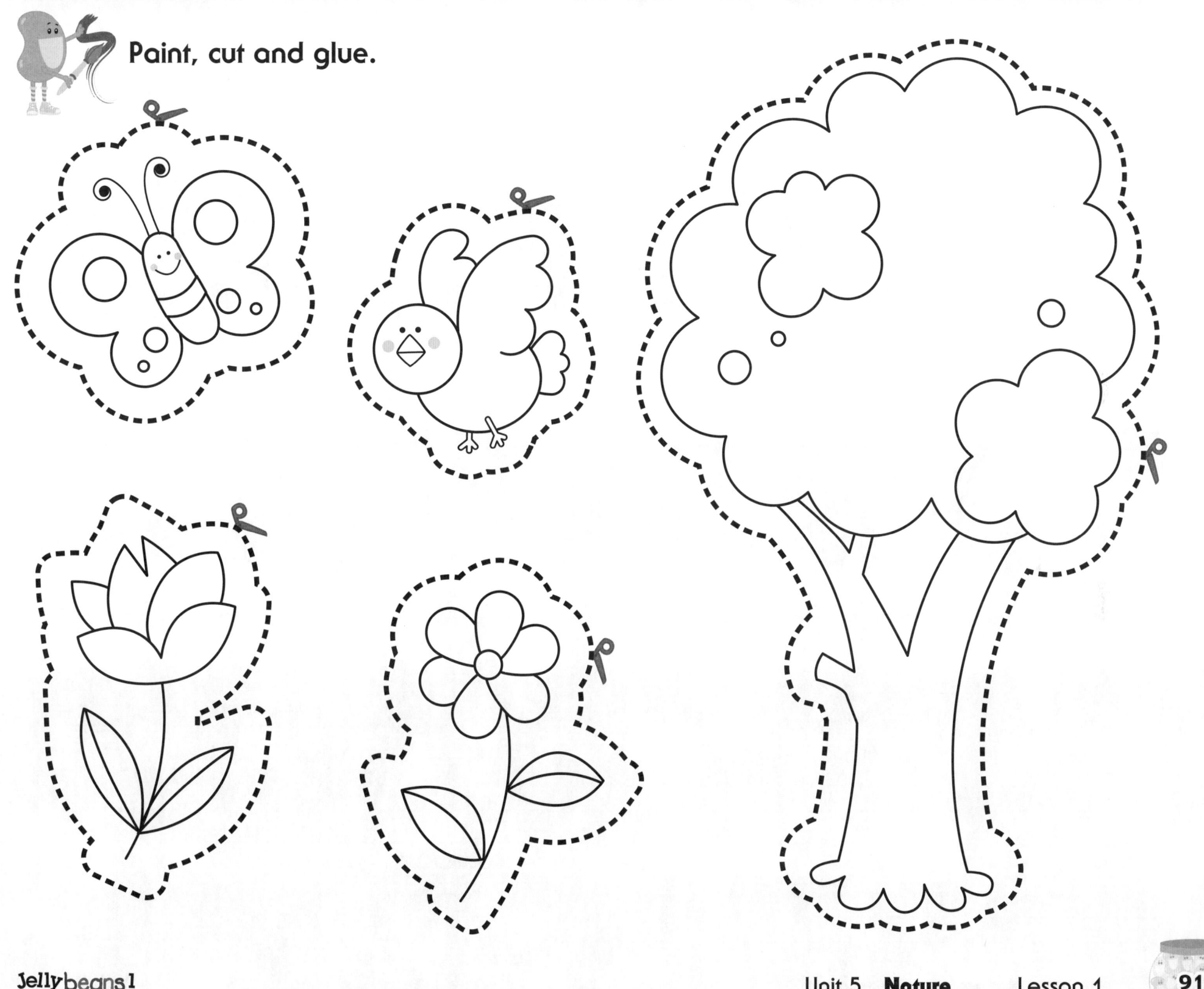

Paint, cut and glue.

Unit 5 **Nature** Lesson 1

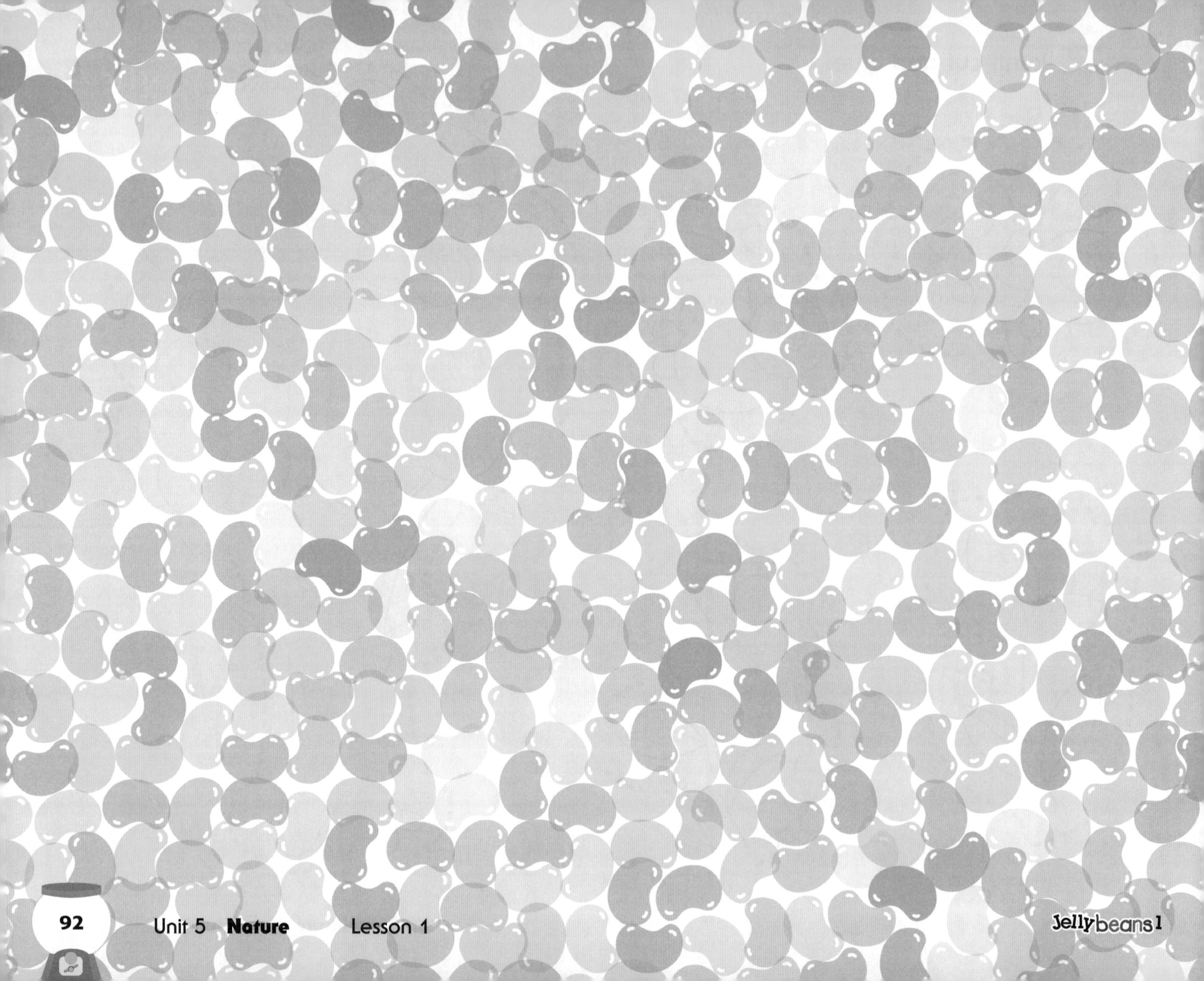

92 Unit 5 **Nature** Lesson 1

Paint, cut and glue.

Jellybeans 1 — Unit 5 **Nature** — Lesson 1 — 93

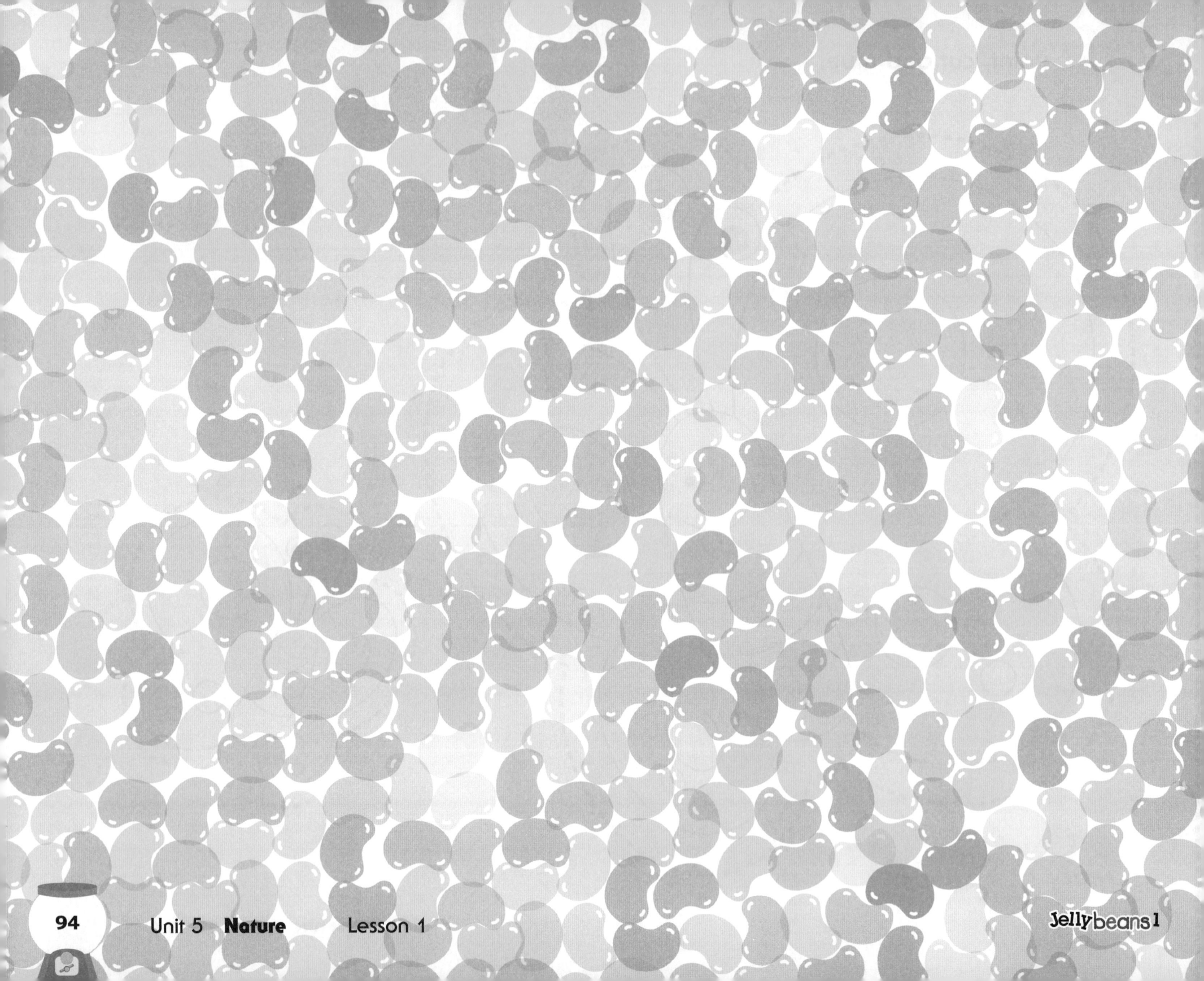

94 Unit 5 **Nature** Lesson 1

Finger-paint and glue.

Jellybeans 1

Unit 5 **Nature** Lesson 2

95

Color, cut and assemble.

Jellybeans 1 — Unit 5 **Nature** Lesson 2 — 97

98 Unit 5 **Nature** Lesson 2

Jellybeans 1

Cut, glue, trace and color.

Unit 6 **Pets**   Lesson 1

100 Unit 6 **Pets** Lesson 1

Color, glue and name.

102 Unit 6 **Pets** Lesson 1

Jellybeans 1

Look and color.

Color, cut and play.

Fold

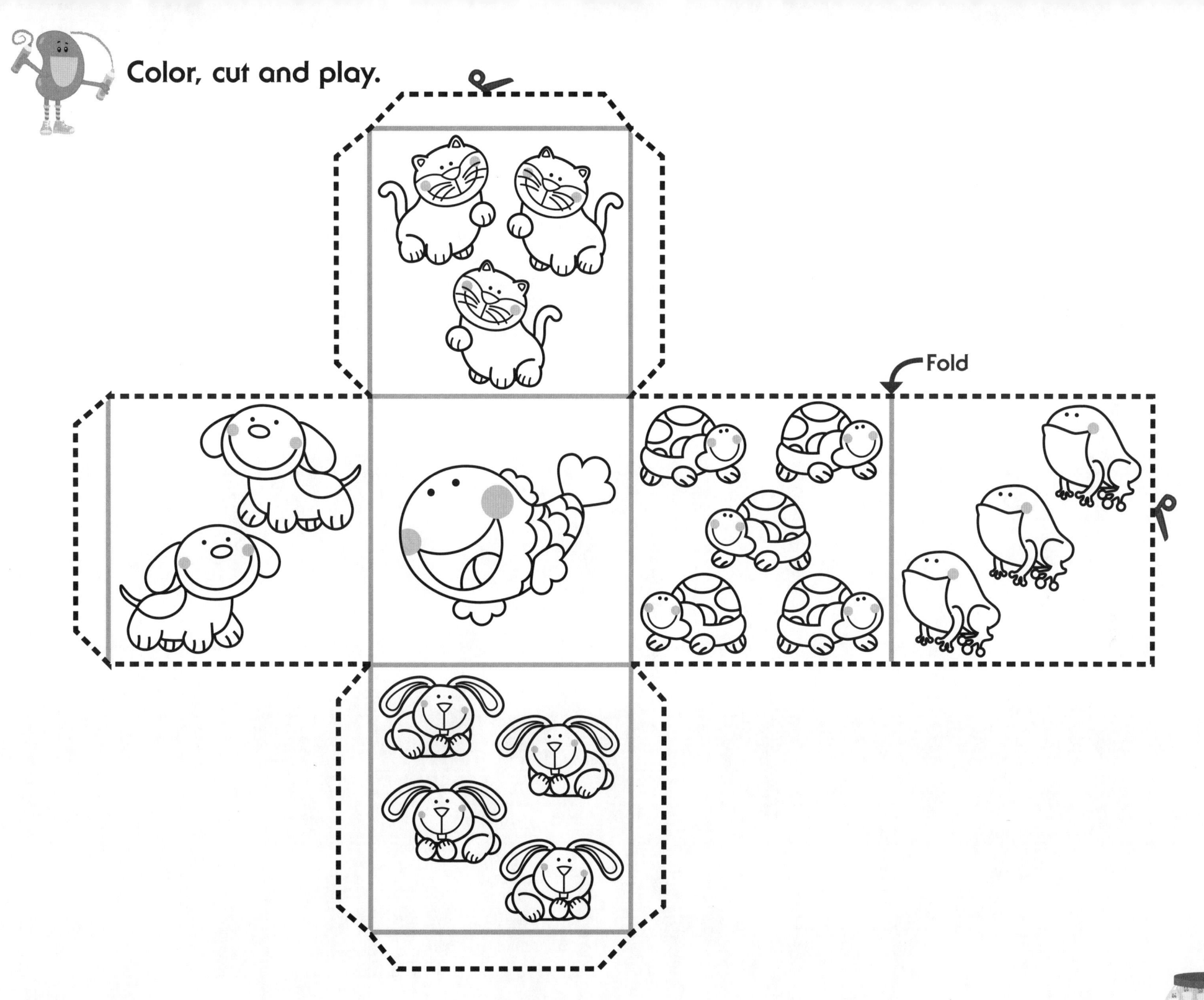

Jellybeans 1 — Unit 6 **Pets** — Lesson 2 — 105

Unit 6 **Pets** Lesson 2

Paint, cut and assemble.

Fold
Fold

Jellybeans 1   Unit 7 **Toys**   Lesson 1

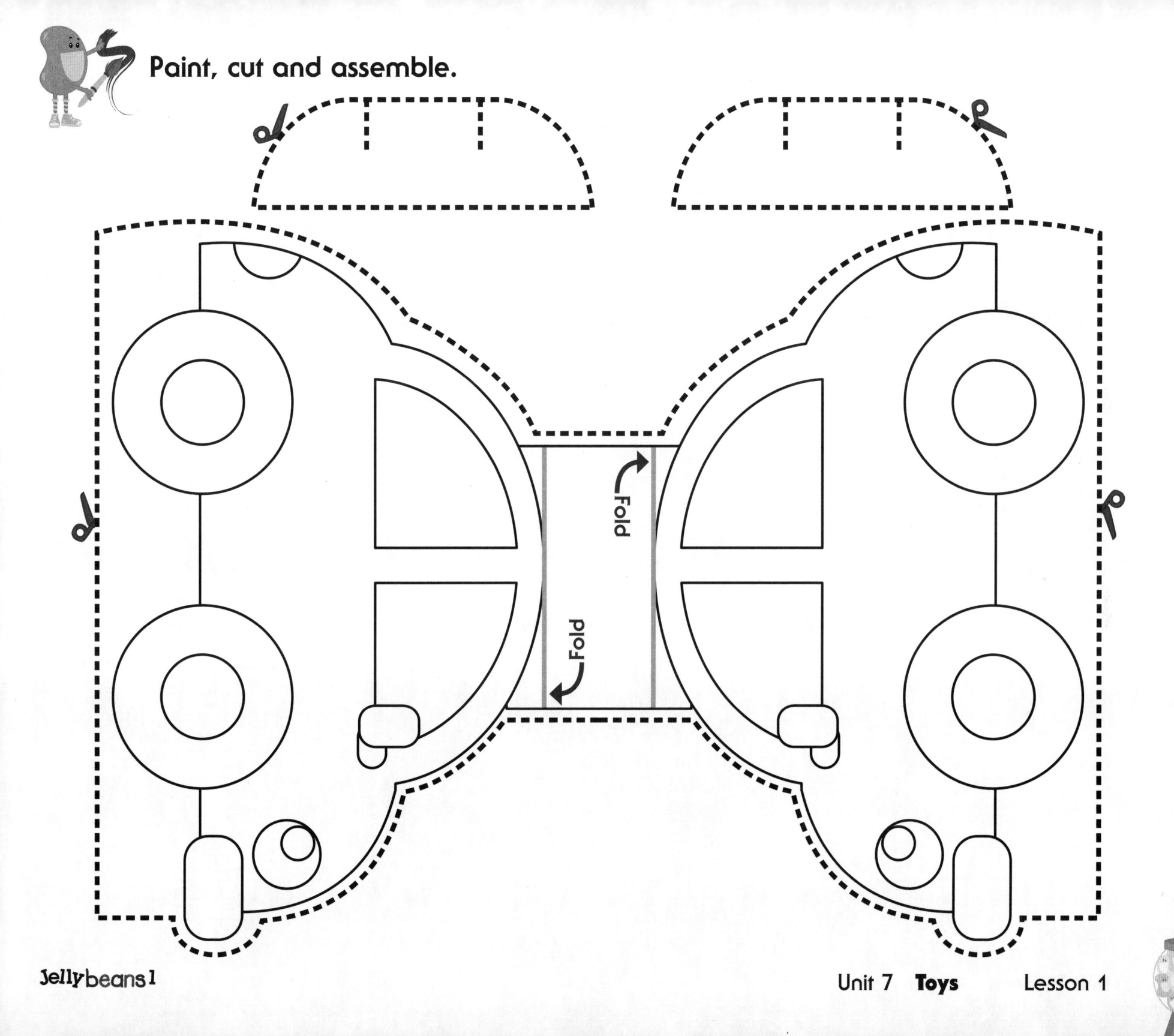

108 Unit 7 **Toys** Lesson 1

Jellybeans 1

Color, cut and play.

Jellybeans 1   Unit 7 **Toys**   Lesson 1   109

110 Unit 7 **Toys** Lesson 1

Jellybeans 1

Look and glue.

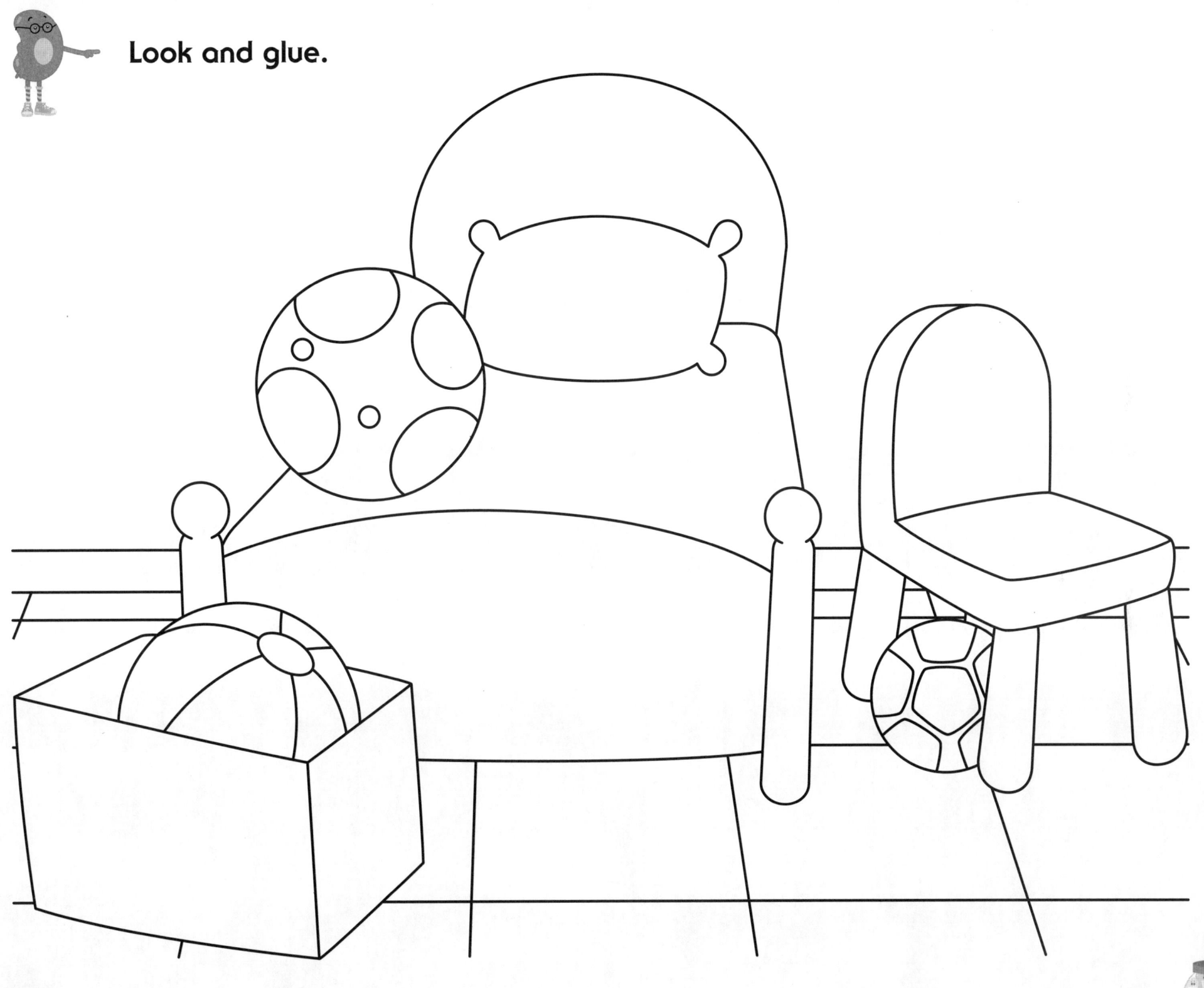

112 Unit 7 **Toys** Lesson 2

Jellybeans!

Color, cut and glue.

Unit 7   **Toys**   Lesson 2

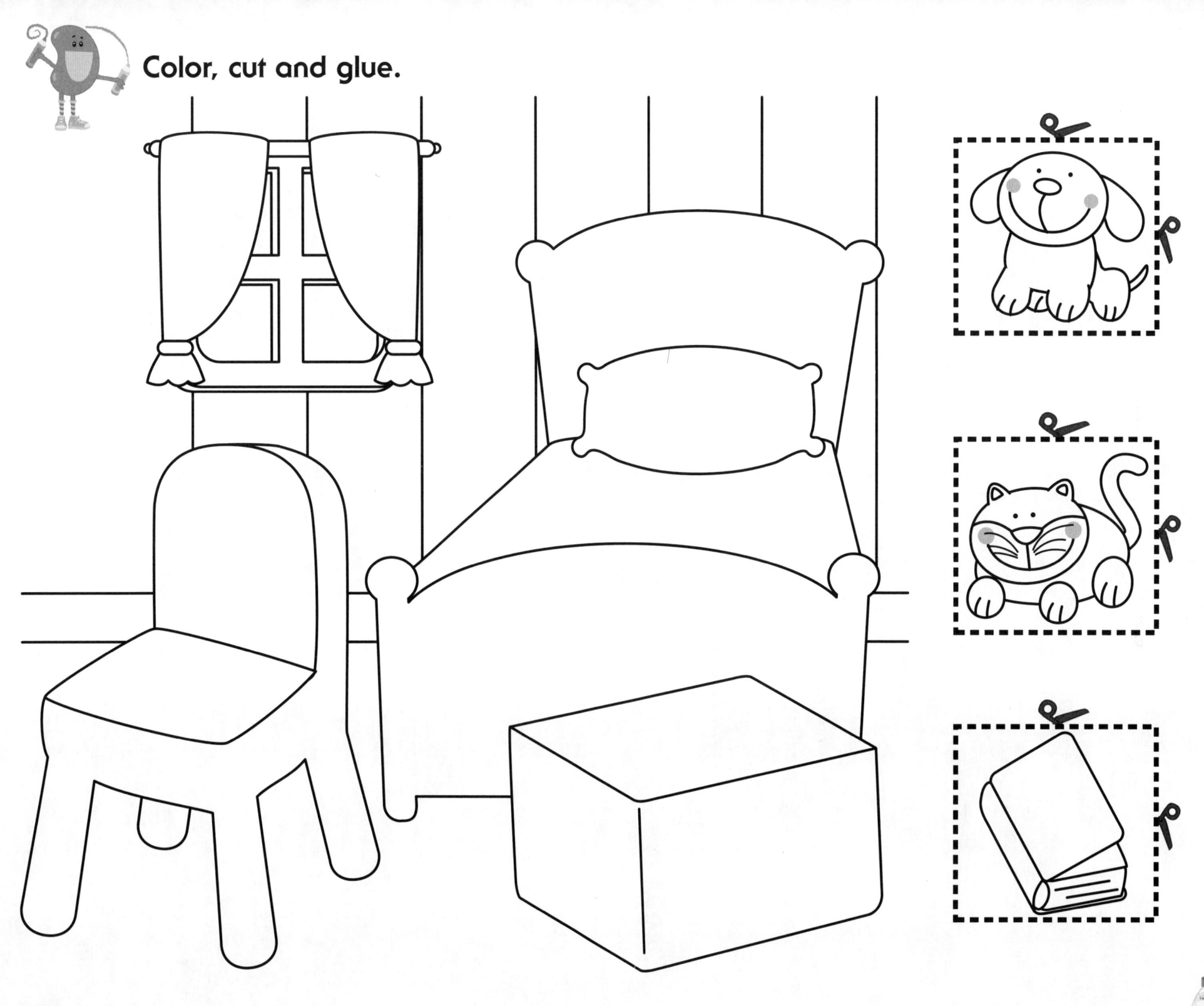

Unit 7 **Toys** Lesson 2

Color, cut and assemble.

Jellybeans 1 — Unit 8 **Food** — Lesson 1 — 115

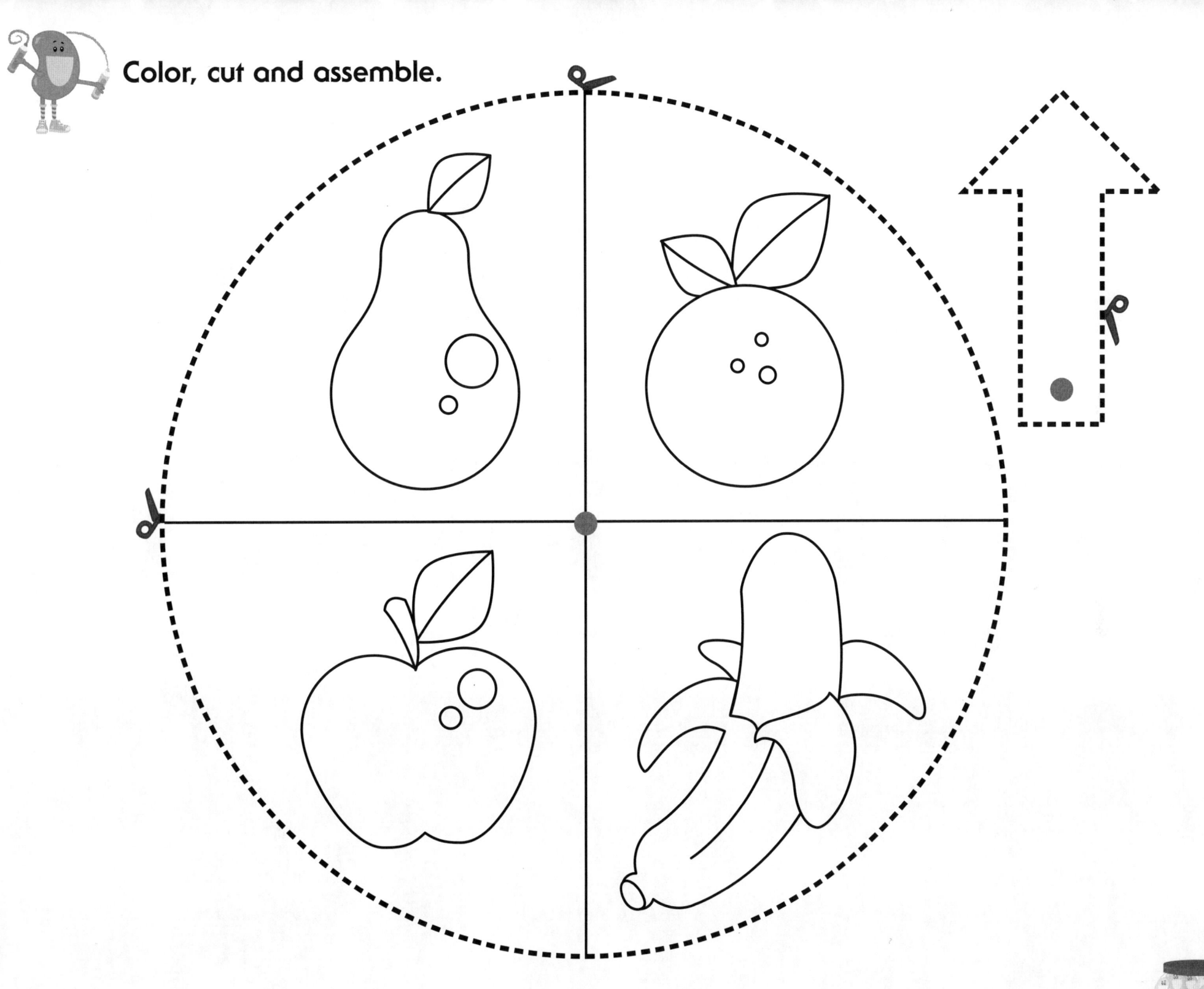

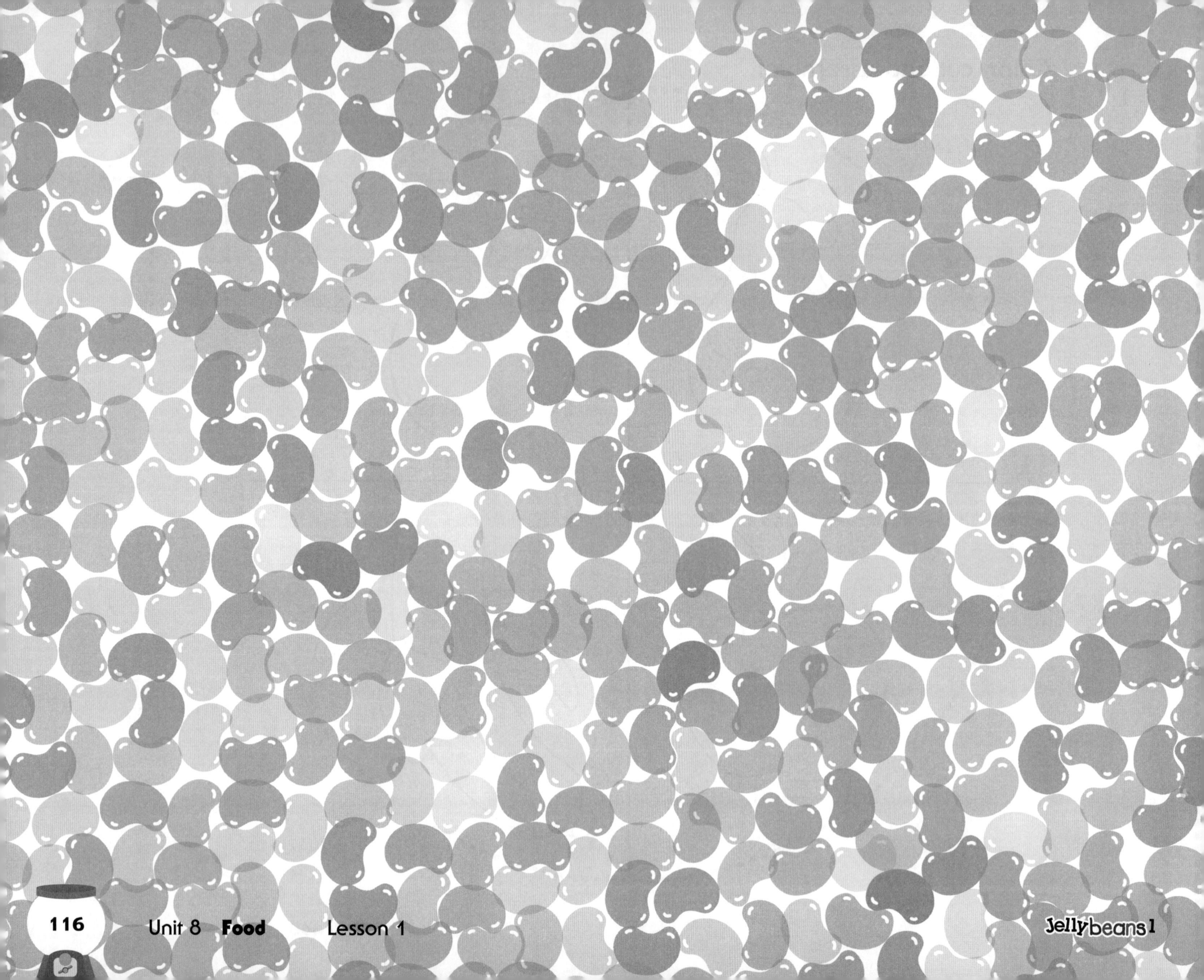

116   Unit 8   **Food**   Lesson 1

Color and cut.

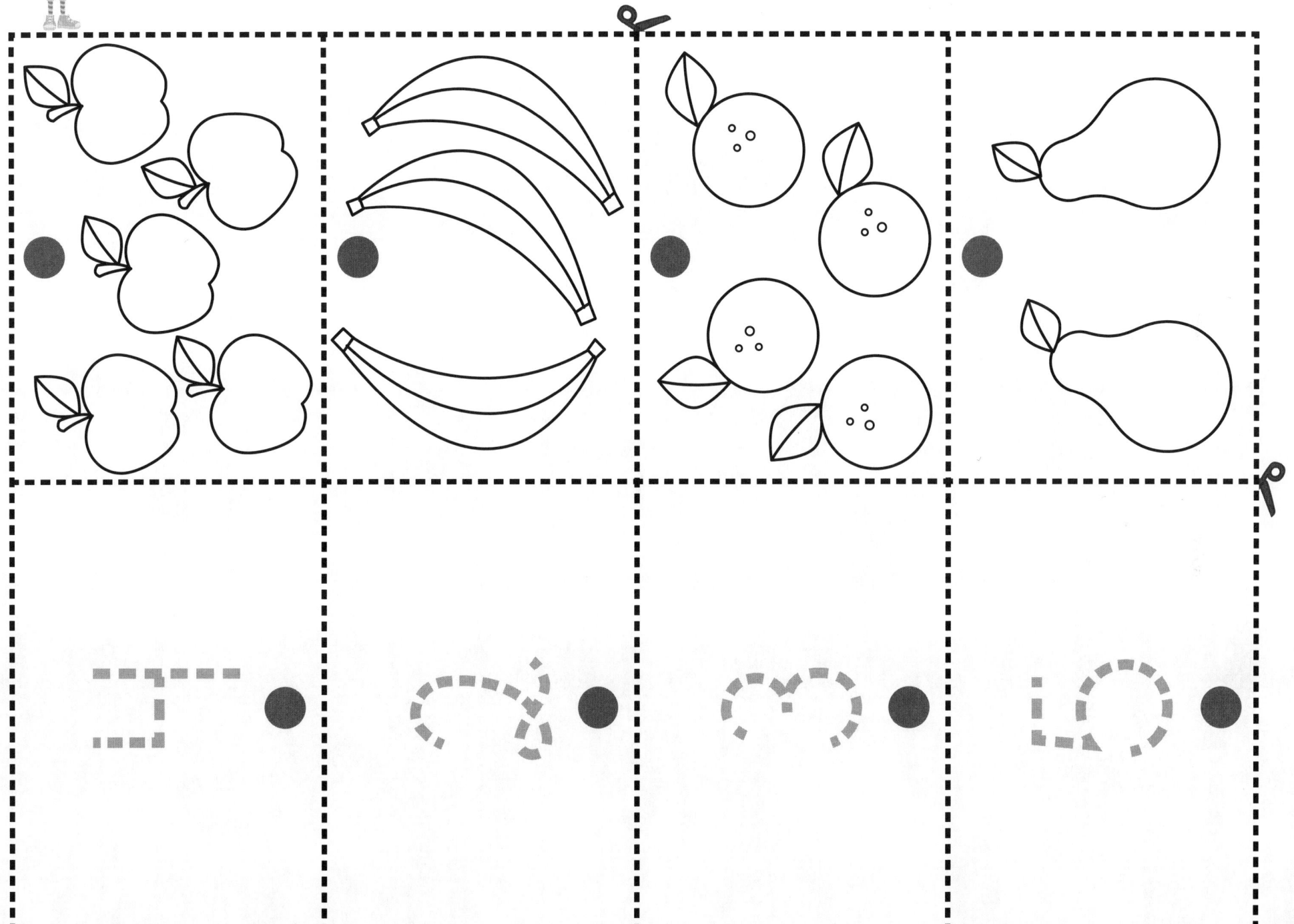

Jellybeans 1 — Unit 8 **Food** — Lesson 1 — 117

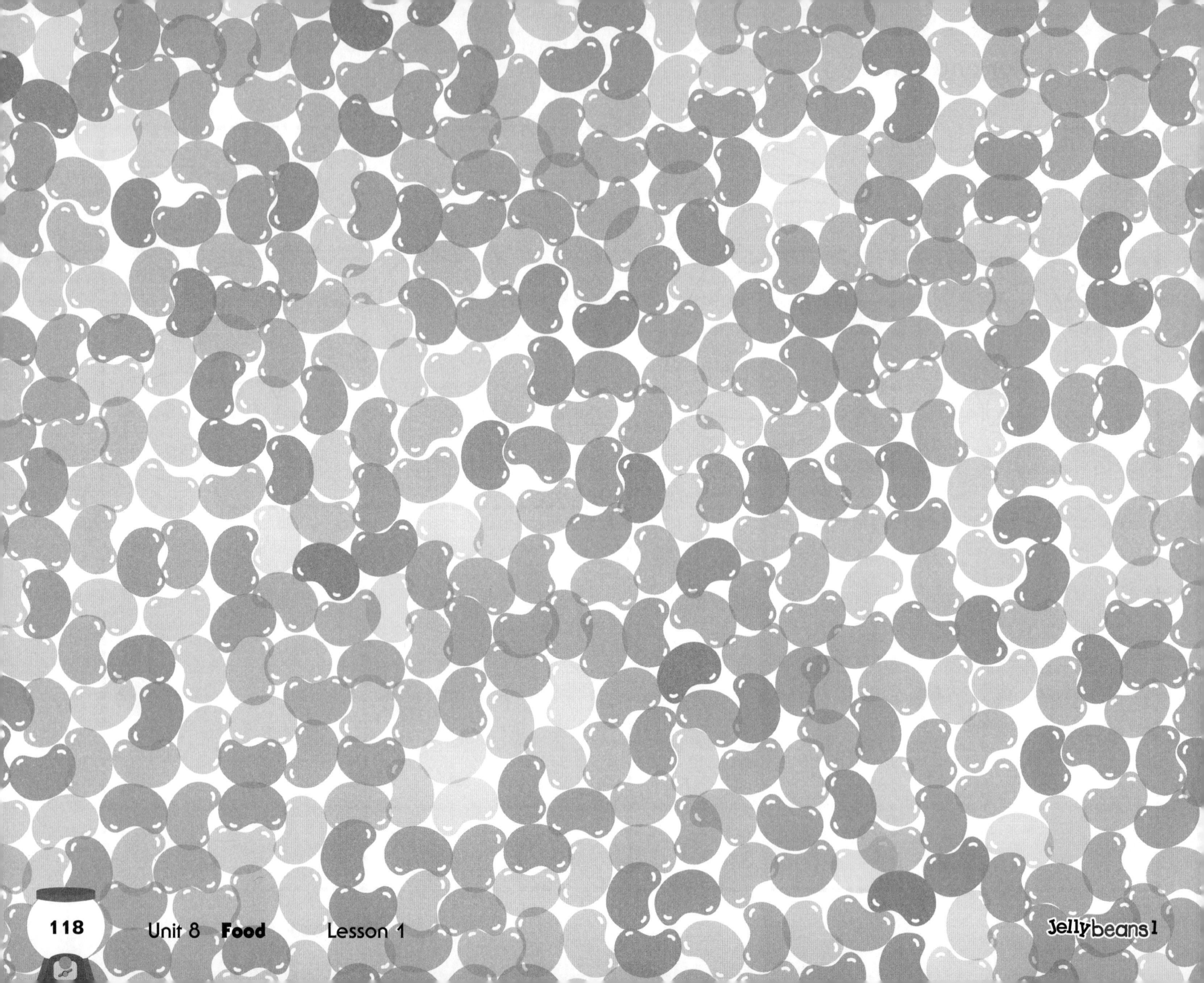

118 Unit 8 **Food** Lesson 1

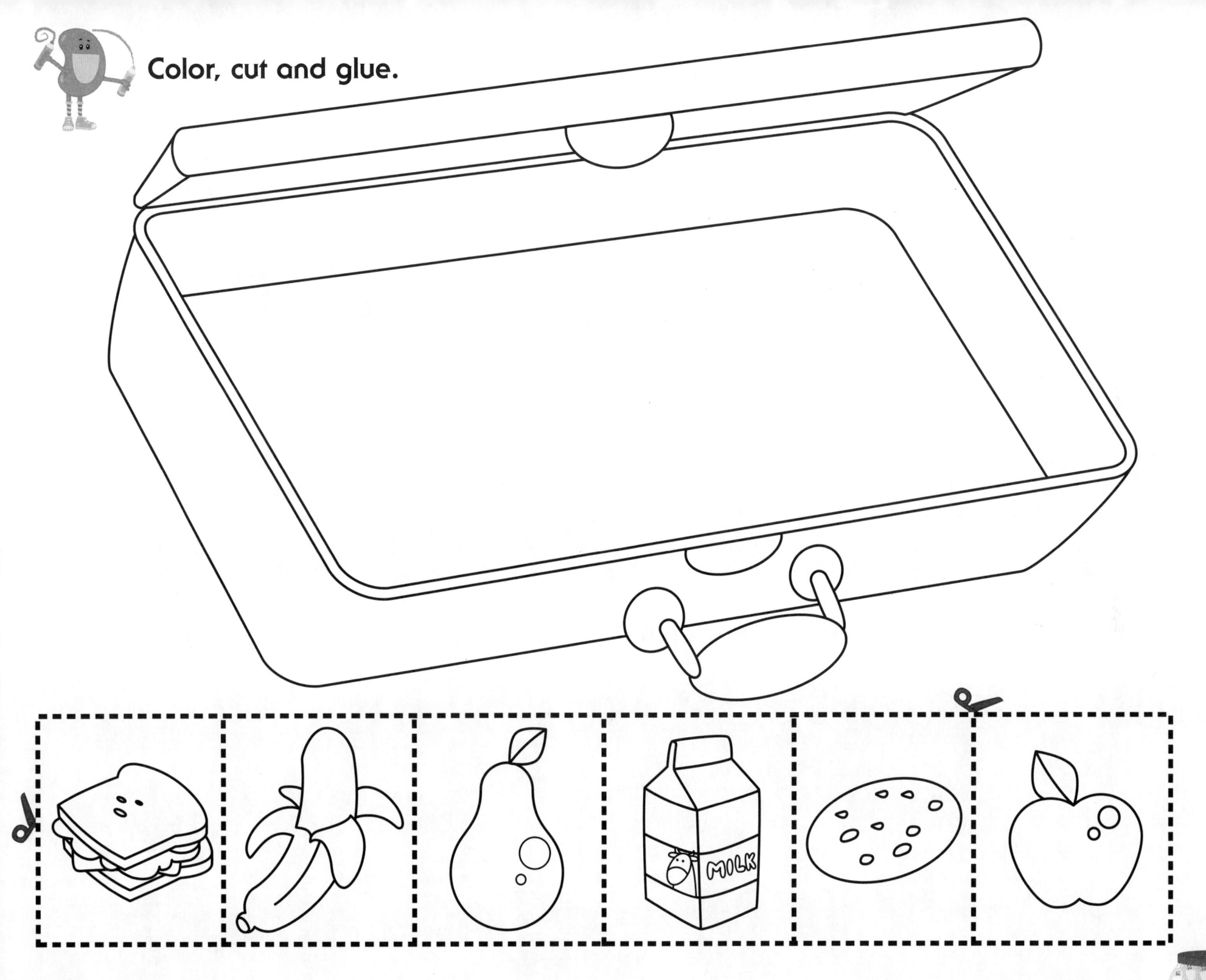

Color, cut and glue.

120 Unit 8 **Food** Lesson 2

Color, cut and glue.

Jellybeans 1 — Unit 8 **Food** — Lesson 2 — 121

122 Unit 8 **Food** Lesson 2　　　Jellybeans 1

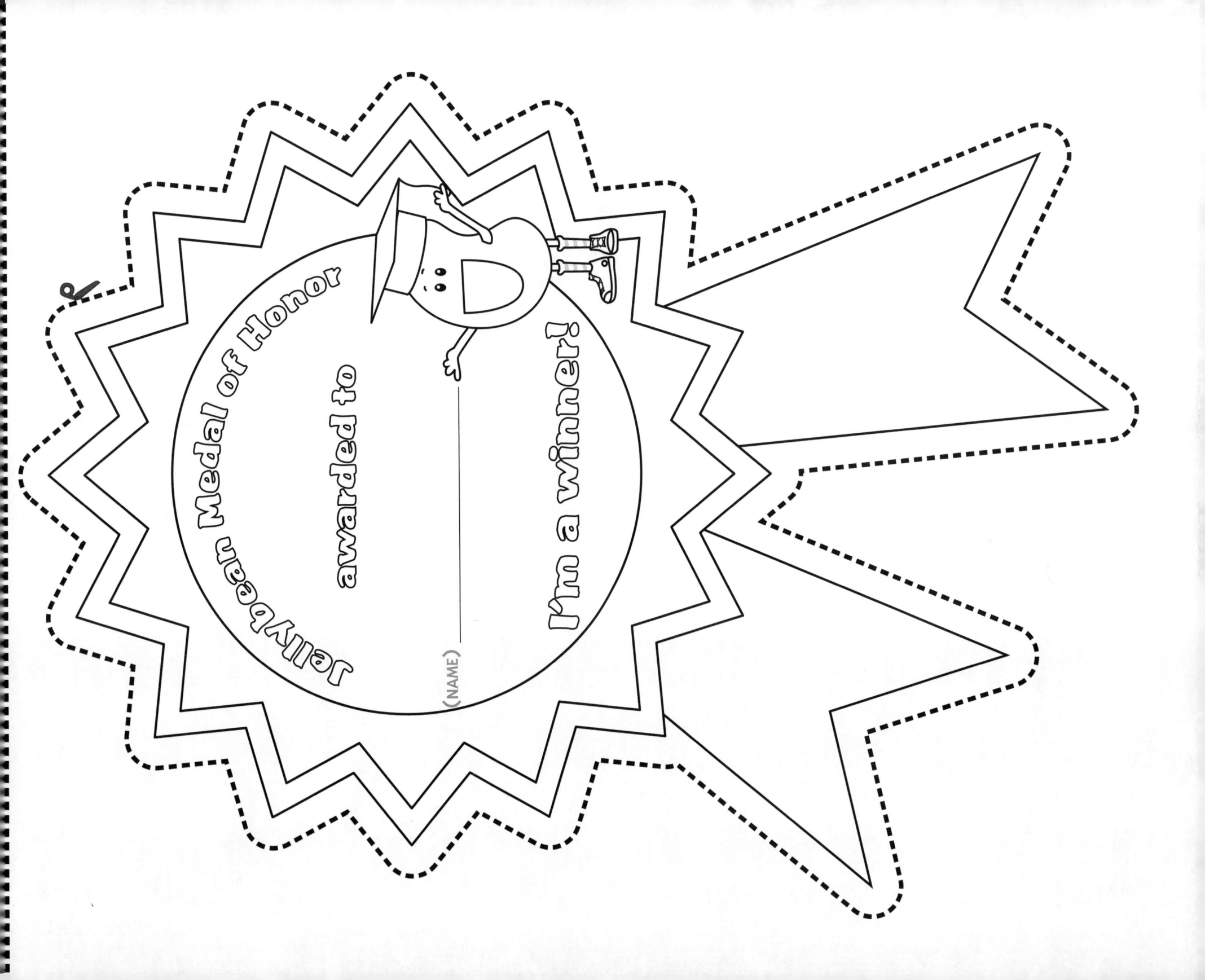

Jellybean Medal of Honor

awarded to

(NAME)

I'm a winner!

Jellybeans 1

Tracks

2	Everybody say hello	13	Take a look around the park
3	Put your finger on the book	14	Let's go to the park
4	This is a table	15	I can point to number 1
5	This is the way we point to red	16	My pets
6	Jellybean count	17	Animal sounds
7	Open, close them	18	Where can it be?
8	Open, open, open your mouth	19	Where is it?
9	Show me happy	20	In your mouth
10	Point to Mommy	21	Point to the apple
11	Point to Grandma	22	Sandwiches are good
12	I love my family		

Jellybeans 1

Jellybeans 1

RICHMOND
58 St. Aldates
Oxford, OX1 1ST
England

Publisher: *Alicia Becker*
Executive Editors: *Alejandra Zapiain, Kimberley Silver*
Proofreaders: *Cristina Navarrete, Jen Braun*

Design Supervisor: *Marisela Pérez*
Design and Art Direction: *Marilú Jiménez*
Cover Design: *Marilú Jiménez*
Cover Illustration: *Raúl García*
DTP and Layout: *Claudia Rocha*
Technical Department: *Daniel Santillán, Edgar Colín, José Luis Ávila, Salvador Pereira*

Illustrations: *Claudia Navarro, Fabiola Graullera, Isabel Arnaud, Javier Montiel, Marissa Arroyo, Teresa Martínez*

First Edition: D.R. © Richmond Publishing, S.A. de C.V., 2008

All rights reserved. No part of this book may be reproduced, stored in a retrieval system or transmitted in any form or by any means, electronic, mechanical, photocopying, recording or otherwise, without prior permission in writing of the publishers.

Every effort has been made to trace the owners of copyright, but if any omissions can be rectified, the publisher will be pleased to make the necessary arrangements.

This Edition: © Editora Moderna Ltda., 2011.
Editor: *Carla Montenegro*
Pedagogical Consultant: *Silvia Teles*
Copy Editor: *Sheila Winckler S. da Silva*
Proofreaders: *Camila Carmo da Silva, Katia Gouveia Vitale, Mariana Mininel de Almeida, Vivian M. Viccino*
Designer: *Gláucia Koller*
Layout: *Yara Campi*

Dados Internacionais de Catalogação na Publicação (CIP)
(Câmara Brasileira do Livro, SP, Brasil)

Salvador, Rebecca Williams
   Jelly beans, 1 : student's book / Rebecca Williams Salvador & Adela Trabolsi. — São Paulo : Moderna, 2011.

   Suplementado pelo manual do professor

   1. Inglês (Educação infantil) I. Trabolsi, Adela. II. Título.

11-04417   CDD-372.21

Índices para catálogo sistemático:
1. Inglês : Educação infantil   372.21

ISBN 978-85-16-07073-1 (LA)
ISBN 978-85-16-07074-8 (LP)

Reprodução proibida. Art.184 do Código Penal e Lei 9.610 de 19 de fevereiro de 1998.
Todos os direitos reservados.

RICHMOND
EDITORA MODERNA LTDA.
Rua Padre Adelino, 758 – Belenzinho
São Paulo – SP – Brasil – CEP 03303-904
Central de atendimento ao usuário: 0800 771 8181
www.richmond.com.br
2020

Impresso no Brasil
Bercrom Gráfica e Editora
Lote: 284562

Jelly beans 1

Stickers

Jellybeans 1

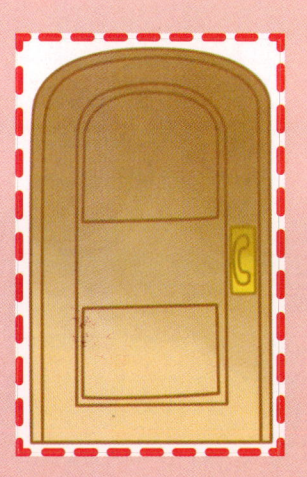

Unit 1 I go to school

Unit 2 **Colors and numbers**

Unit 3 My face

Unit 4 **My family**

Jellybeans 1   Unit 5   Nature

Unit 6 Pets

Unit 6 **Pets**

Unit 7 Toys

Unit 8 Food

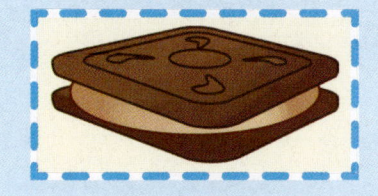